G000270966

ENDORSEME

This is the real story of the life of a Palestinian Christian Arab woman growing up as a refugee in the Levant after the formation of the state of Israel, and God's faithfulness in protecting her. Afaf and her family lost their roots, but her mother's faith and determination brought them through their childhood to rely on God for his unfailing protection. Afaf's faith grows throughout her life despite numerous challenges, with God giving her guidance and courage as to how and where she should live her life. God provides for her every need – "a handful of pennies" – God's grace is always sufficient.

Dr Moira Pinkney
Paediatrician and General Practitioner

In this fascinating and moving narrative, the author recounts her journey as a Palestinian Christian from her roots in Israel, then through the civil wars of the Lebanon as a refugee, and finally to life in England. Throughout the many moves, the persistent question of personal identity remains a constant theme, and the author describes how ultimately she has found her identity in Christ. This powerful account is for all those interested in refugees and in finding answers to the challenges we all face in finding God's way through the storms of life.

Dr Denis Alexander
Emeritus Fellow of St. Edmund's College, Cambridge

This is a remarkable book – powerful, poignant and timely. The author, Afaf, vividly describes living through some of the most significant and tumultuous events in the recent history of the Middle East – being made a refugee as a child in 1948, "sleeping our first night on a concrete floor under the stars", living through some of the unspeakable horrors of Lebanon's long and bloody civil war and donning a gas mask in Jerusalem in the first Gulf War. Her struggles to find her identity as a Palestinian Christian, and with the proposals of well-meaning friends to find her a husband, are told with honesty, faith and courage.

It seems strangely fitting that Afaf should now be involved in caring for refugees from Syria where once as a child she queued to collect her family's rations. "This refugee's story," she writes, "is my testimony to God's goodness, love and dependability." It is a profound testimony.

The Revd Peter Crooks MBE
Served with churches and communities across the Middle East, in Beirut, Damascus and most recently Aden, and also in Jerusalem where he was Dean of the Anglican Cathedral.

Onwards and Upwards Publishers

4 The Old Smithy
London Road
Rockbeare
EX5 2EA
United Kingdom
www.onwardsandupwards.org

First edition, published in the United Kingdom by Onwards and Upwards Publishers Ltd. (2022).

ISBN: 978-1-78815-983-8
Typeface: Sabon LT

A Handful of Pennies

A refugee's lifelong quest for
identity and peace

Afaf Musallam

O&U
Onwards & Upwards

ABOUT THE AUTHOR

Afaf Musallam belongs to three countries. Born in Haifa, Palestine, she was forced to become a refugee as a child in the 1948 war. She eventually managed to settle in Lebanon, where she gained a higher education, but was subsequently forced to flee again due to the destruction of the country's civil war. Eventually, the UK became Afaf's second adopted country. Although Afaf's journey has been a difficult one, her early encounter with Christ set her on a course towards finding her identity, along with peace, joy and a sense of contentment. Throughout her life, she has seen numerous answers to prayer and has experienced God's continual hand of protection. Afaf co-founded the Jaffa Orchard Community Coffee shop, a Christian venture in Bedford, which ran from 2001 to 2016. She is now involved in interpreting and befriending Arabic-speaking refugees in Bedford.

To contact the author, please write to:

Afaf Musallam
c/o Onwards and Upwards Publishers
4 The Old Smithy
London Road
Rockbeare
EX5 2EA

Or send an email to:

afafmusallam1@gmail.com

This book is dedicated to a wonderful praying mother, Wadia Habiby Musallam. She gave everything she had, and I owe her so much; she never gave up on me, she prayed for me and she was my guiding light on my long journey.

It is also dedicated to my precious sisters and their families, Siham, Iptissam and Huda. Without them being around, I would not have made it. To all my friends, church family and extended family, I am indebted to you all. You have enriched my life by your willingness to share your friendships. To you all I say a big thank you for allowing me to be part of your lives and leading me to find forgiveness, peace and joy.

A Handful of Pennies

CONTENTS

A Handful of Pennies

FOREWORD BY REV. COLIN CHAPMAN

As someone who has known Afaf for many years, it's a great pleasure to commend her very personal and inspiring story. This is a powerful testimony of how she has experienced the love and protection of God from her earliest years as a Palestinian refugee, moving through Jordan and Syria, then settling in Lebanon and finally in the UK. The intriguing title points to many moving stories of how she and her family have experienced God's providential care – stories that sceptics could hardly dismiss as pure chance or coincidence.

This is also a moving account of someone struggling with issues about identity. How does Afaf hold together her awareness of being born a Palestinian, then living in Lebanon for thirty-five years and gaining Lebanese citizenship, and finally emigrating to the UK and getting a British passport? How can she possibly be Palestinian, Lebanese and British at the same time? And how does her Christian faith help her to understand who she is?

Afaf's story also has a powerful message about forgiveness and reconciliation. She has never forgotten the experience of leaving her home in Haifa on a British army lorry in May 1948 and being taken to the West Bank. But she writes of returning with her mother to Haifa in 1991 and introducing herself to the present Jewish owners of their family home. She has no bitterness or resentment over all that has happened, but only a quiet confidence in a loving and powerful God – a God who is the Lord of history and at the same time cares for all his people as individuals. This must be the starting point for Christians who want to be peacemakers in a conflict that has lasted for many decades.

Readers of this story will certainly want to join with Afaf and the Psalmist to *'thank the LORD for his steadfast love'* (Psalm 107:8, ESV).

The Reverend Colin Chapman
Formerly Regional Secretary for the Middle East
IFES (International Fellowship of Evangelical Students)

ACKNOWLEDGEMENTS

I would like to extend my sincere appreciation and thanks to many friends and family members who contributed, encouraged and helped me in writing my story, especially to:

Alison and Chris Walley
Joy Denny
Claire Pound-Corner
Scott Mccarty
Paul Sands
Helen Hall
Luke Jeffery
Leah-Maarit Jeffery
Howard Brown
Siham Brown

PROLOGUE

The year was 2020 and it was an unusually hot day for England. I parked the car in a street near the grocery shop and looked left and right; no cars were coming, so I crossed. In the middle of the road, three coins were embedded in the soft tarmac. I bent down and gingerly prised out a 50p and two 20p coins. I was amazed, not only that they were not on the pavement, assuming they had fallen out of someone's pocket, but that they were stuck as a result of cars running over them. I added the 90p to my street-collection box.

Some years ago, I had been on holiday in the south of Spain with two friends. The three of us were walking on a completely deserted sandy beach when I almost stepped on two small round objects shining brightly in the sun. I bent down and picked them up. To my amazement, I was looking at two white coins. Not only was there not a piece of litter on this spotless beach, but there was nobody else there apart from us, and none of us had dropped any coins. Now, many years later, I wonder: a deserted beach with two coins on top of the sand – why?

In August 2019, I picked up another coin from the rear of a supermarket in Bedford, on a little used shortcut. It was a beautiful day, the sun was shining and I needed the exercise, so I walked there via the river. I had not written anything of my memoirs for the last two days but, as if on cue, I picked up another 1p coin. Was there Someone reminding me to carry on writing *A Handful of Pennies*? I came back home, sat in the garden and typed on my laptop for an hour and a half until the chill forced me inside. Previously, when these 'findings' had taken place, I had thought nothing of them: 'Coincidences,' I had assured myself. But it can't be... So many of them? The regularity of their happening was so frequent – so unusual, to say the least. As of today, I have accumulated more than a few pounds in the 'found box'.

Why am I telling you all this? Because now I know the significance of all these coin findings. I started writing my story more than eight years ago. Every time I stopped writing, I found another coin, as if reminding me not to forget to tell the story of *A Handful of Pennies*. That was just the beginning. Would you like to hear my story?

It begins in 1948, in Palestine...

1

The Nightmare Journey

HAIFA, PALESTINE – 1948

The root of what was happening in Palestine in 1948 began with the demise of the Ottoman Empire. In 1918, the Ottoman Army was defeated by the British, who got rid of them with the help of a number of secret promises. The first: they promised the Arabs independence if they would rebel against the Ottomans. The Arabs duly did. The second: they made an agreement with the French that they would divide the entire Middle East into areas of influence. Which they did. The third: they promised prominent British Jews that they would support a Jewish homeland in Palestine, and they did. Of course, these three promises contradicted each other and set the stage for the ongoing fighting between the indigenous Palestinian population and the newcomers. This culminated in one of our modern-day human tragedies.

It was a sad day in May 1948 when we left our home on Mount Carmel, Haifa. There had been a night of fierce fighting between Palestinians and Jewish fighters who had come to Palestine aboard ships fleeing Europe. The British Mandate army found themselves in the middle, and tried desperately to keep the peace but failed miserably.

The fighting had intensified significantly in and around the region where we lived. On that eventful day, we saw my uncle racing up the thirty steps to our house on Abbas Street, shouting out Mother's name. Almost breathless, he stumbled through the door.

'Wadia, thank God you're all right. You need to get out – *now*.'

'But I need to pack some things,' she said desperately.

'Quickly, then. You'll be able to leave the fighting zone, but you've got to get to St Luke's Church straight away. The vicar has arranged it all and there are trucks waiting at the church. The British Army is going to take all the Palestinian families from the church to somewhere safe.'

There was chaos and panic as Mother gathered us girls together and told us to get ready to leave. Siham was twelve, Iptissam six, I was five and our youngest sister Huda was only two. Mother frantically gathered things to take with us and started packing a small suitcase. I stood there clutching my Red Riding Hood doll in my arms, watching her pack. She turned her face away for a moment and I sneaked my doll in. Mother immediately spotted the doll and, without saying a word, removed it from the suitcase. I sneaked it in again, and again she removed it. Silently, I stood there, tears streaming down my face, clutching my doll to my chest, fearing that Red Riding Hood was not coming with me. The suitcase was forced shut. We all stood there with the suitcase and the mattress ready to go. I looked sadly at Red Riding Hood sitting on the table all by herself for the last time. I left without my beloved doll.

Mother marched us out of the house carrying her handbag on her arm. It contained the few Palestinian pounds she owned and her wedding ring. She locked the door behind us and very, very slowly, carrying the heavy mattress and suitcase between us, we manoeuvred the stony steps down. Halfway down, we stopped briefly at our neighbours' house, and left our house key with them for safe keeping until we returned.

We carried on walking for another ten minutes until we reached St Luke's Church and met up with my uncle's family and others who were also leaving. In front of us stood seven grey British army trucks, ready to move out. People were frightened, excited and talked in loud voices. Some milled around as they loaded the luggage onto the trucks. Once that was done, my uncle helped his family and then our family to climb on. I was a thin five-year-old girl, so he lifted me up, passed me from hand to hand and then placed me on the mattress beside a dazed Mother, who had my little sister Huda in her lap.

All this happened so fast. We were all on the trucks now, and slowly, slowly, the trucks with their human and non-human cargo moved out; down Mount Carmel Road and onto the sea road before heading inland. All eyes looked back and saw the calm sea behind as if waving us goodbye. We saw Haifa for the last time as it vanished from sight. At that precise moment no one realised that our beloved Haifa would be no more than a memory etched on our thoughts.

Unvoiced questions were going through everyone's mind. Fear was visible on people's faces, but no one spoke. Where were we going? What would happen to us? Mother sat motionless on the mattress, her body responding to the swaying of the truck from side to side. She held tightly to my younger sister in her lap. My father had passed away two years earlier after an accident, so she had four girls aged two to twelve to look after by herself. How was she going to cope?

We fled Haifa so suddenly. In Mother's anxiety to escape, she had forgotten to pick up our most important papers: our identity cards and birth certificates. She thought, like everyone else, that in a month's time when all the fighting died down, we would come back to the safety of our homes and resume our normal lives in Haifa.

The tragic reality was that we never returned; we were never allowed back. With no identification to say who we were, the fate of our homeless, stateless family was sealed: we were refugees.

2

The Refugees

AMMAN, JORDAN

The British army trucks, after a sixty-mile horrendous drive from Haifa, dumped us in Nablus. 'That's it,' the soldiers announced. So we all got off.

Someone found and paid a local truck driver willing to drive us the rest of the journey to the Jordanian capital, Amman. Night had fallen and we were on an open truck, standing room only, for forty miles. The road was treacherously dark, so we arrived traumatised both physically and emotionally, exhausted and numb from the day's harrowing events. We were just a few more bedraggled, frightened and hungry families among hundreds of others already there. The scene that greeted us was heartbreaking: the very old and the very young, some fit but others obviously unwell. The pitiful mass of people moved on, doing what the camp officials told them to do, except Mother, who refused point blank to go to the refugee camp on the outskirts of town. She pleaded with the official:

'Please sir, can we not go to the camp tonight as we are expecting friends to meet the family here tomorrow?'

He looked at us for a moment and then pointed to an unfinished three-storey building.

'You can camp there tonight, if you wish,' he said.

We thanked the kind-hearted official, and with my uncle's family we carried our mattresses and suitcases and went up the stairs to the first floor of the roofless building. Exhausted, we slept our first night on the concrete floor under the cover of a starlit sky.

We stayed there two more nights, and our next shelter was a single room mud shack with only a small tap for drinking water. To pay the rent, Mother had to sell her wedding ring. The Jordanian authorities issued us with our first refugee cards and with these we got our daily bread, but that was all. Fortunately, Mother was a qualified nurse and she was able to earn a little money by giving injections. Wherever we went, we were recognised by these cards as refugees. No one wanted us; all wanted to get rid of us, as we were a burden to all. We belonged nowhere and owned nothing, except the clothes that were on our backs. We did, however, have Mother's faith in God that gave us our security.

Because of lack of facilities where we lived, we had to visit the Turkish baths for our weekly bath. These were communal baths used by anyone who had the few coins to pay for them. We arrived at this unusual round building, hot and dirty, having passed through the humid streets downtown. As we entered, I was blinded by the hot steam that filled the big circular hall, and the refreshing smell of clean Nabulsi soap reached my nostrils. A big marble pond adorned the middle of the hall. Tucked in around the walls were six benches attached to six small alcoves beyond where people washed. Rays of sunlight streamed through small steamed-up glass windows in the domed ceiling and filled the hall with light. I was so excited to have my first bath at this unusual bathhouse.

After an hour I emerged refreshed and clean, but alas, as soon as we rejoined the crowded streets outside, that sensation deserted me!

An amazing answer to prayer

Mother belonged to the Anglican church, but had joined the new Brethren church in Haifa before she left. This church had now moved to Amman, and its members gave us a lot of moral and practical support during these six difficult months. They helped us move from the shack into better accommodation. Roy Whitman and his wife, founders of this assembly, had contacts with The British Syrian Mission School in Baalbeck, Lebanon. The principal was a friend of theirs and they also had a cousin who was a teacher there.

September was upon us and we were not registered in any school. Time was short as schools started to re-open. Mother was getting more and more agitated, as she was increasingly concerned about our schooling. Regularly, she would complain about the dire situation we were in and wanting us to be registered in a school. My uncle often reminded her that she should be thankful to the Lord and content that she had a roof over her head and not a tent. Not deterred, she asked the Whitmans to write a letter to their principal friend and to their cousin at the Baalbeck school, to ask if there was an opening for her four girls to attend the school that year.

Days passed and there was still no answer to the Whitmans' letter. Hope slowly faded, but she never gave up or stopped praying, pleading with the Lord for our future. One evening Mother missed her evening church meeting. Exhausted mentally and physically from the anxieties and responsibilities of the family, she stretched out beside us as we slept on mattresses on the floor. Mother managed to fall asleep but woke up suddenly, feeling an urgent need to pray. She gently woke up my eldest sister, Siham, and both sat up, opened the Bible and read from it. Mother's eyes focused on Philippians 3:1 (EHV): *'Finally, my brethren, rejoice in the Lord.'* She could not read any more as a strong gust of wind flung her and Siham back to the floor. They both cried, laughed and praised God at the same time, saying:

'Thank you, Lord Jesus.'

Mother hugged my sister and told her that our problems were at an end. She did not know where, how or when, but she had the assurance that our sufferings and hardships in Amman were over.

A week later, Mother and my aunt were sitting outside in the sunshine, when my uncle came running towards them with a telegram in his hand. It was the long-awaited answer to the Whitmans' letter. Unfortunately, it did not make sense as the translation between Arabic and English had distorted the meaning. That was rectified when the post office issued the original message, and there was great rejoicing: not only were we accepted at the school but, in addition, they needed a matron and offered Mother the job. The first answer to her prayers.

The next big worry was how to get from Amman in Jordan to Baalbeck in Lebanon. To hire a taxi was out of the question as we could not afford it, so she would need to make a five-hour bus journey over treacherous mountainous terrain with four girls on her own. Her trust in God did not waiver, and her faith and prayers were rewarded.

Mother's plan was to break the long bus journey with a stop in Damascus, where she would leave two-year-old Huda with her brother Adib's family, who had settled there after fleeing Haifa. Huda was too young to be with us at the boarding school.

But amazingly, soon afterwards, Uncle Karim, Mother's other brother, who owned a taxi firm in Damascus, showed up unexpectedly in Amman. When Mother asked him why he had come, his answer was:

'I don't know why, but I had an urge to come and see you.'

'Do you have clients you brought to Amman or clients to take back to Damascus?'

'None at all,' he replied

We all marvelled at the timing of all these events. Instead of a rickety bus, we travelled in the most comfortable private taxi and had the company of my dear uncle as the driver.

We arrived at the Jordanian border, where we got out of the car and presented our refugee papers at the checkpoint. The Jordanian border police warned us in no uncertain voice and manner:

'We will allow you to leave Jordan as refugees, but if the Syrian border police refuse you entry into Syria, we will never welcome you back into Jordan.'

What would happen to us then? Mother and my older sister did not contemplate these thoughts but believed in the God who had brought us so far. They prayed and trusted God.

There was no going back now, so we got in the car, uncle drove us across no-man's land and entered Syria at Deraa. The Syrian border police checked our papers: the school invitation telegram and letter. They asked us questions about our destination and when they were satisfied that our destination was Baalbeck in Lebanon, they welcomed the refugee family into Syria. How could I forget! We were on our way to a new country and a new future.

I was guided by a mother who possessed an incredibly strong faith. It was so tangible that it became part of her everyday life. This faith became ingrained on my mind, impacted my unwilling life and became my reality later on.

3

Faith and Citizenship

BAALECK AND BEIRUT, LEBANON – 1950

We spent a few days in Damascus getting ready and saying our goodbyes to two-year-old Huda. Then we got on the bus destined for the school in Baalbeck. It took the creaking, puffing old bus three hours to go over the forty miles of rugged and dangerous mountain roads. The four of us arrived at the school exhausted after the rough journey, but relieved, happy and full of hope.

As we entered the town we saw an imposing two-storey, red-tiled-roof building hugging the main road. This was our destination, The British Mission School. Opposite was the famous Palmyra Hotel, established in 1874 and still open today. Among the famous people who stayed there were Ella Fitzgerald and Charles de Gaulle. The school was built very much in a French Middle Eastern architectural style and its red roof tiles could be seen from miles around. Sadly, the school disappeared years later as it fell victim to the widening of Baalbeck's roads. Baalbeck is 1,183 metres above sea level, nestling in the fertile Bekaa valley between the Lebanon and Anti-Lebanon mountain ranges. It is also a UNESCO World Heritage Site as it has two of the largest, grandest Roman temples, The Temple of Jupiter and The Temple of Bacchus.

I was so excited on entering and seeing the beautiful building with its flower gardens and realised that at last this was going to be home. This was where I was going to live and go to school. Until then, the only school I had attended was the Anglican British School Kindergarten in Haifa, where my aunt was head of department – and that had been only for a week before fleeing Haifa.

Miss Freda Button, the headmistress, welcomed us to the school. Its teachers were both British missionaries and local staff. Mother settled in her job as the all-girls boarding school matron, while we joined the boarders. The school followed the British curriculum of study instead of the Lebanese / Palestinian / Middle Eastern system.

My early years were dogged by ill health. I was born prematurely at eight months, and shortages of food and medicine during the Second World War and the conflict in Palestine meant that I was underweight, frail and sick. I was five when we arrived at the school, but my thin legs would not take me up the seventeen steps to the boarders' dormitory, so I had to be carried up. At that age, I don't think I was aware of my infirmities and the effect they would have on my life later on. I just knew that I was blessed to be in this boarding school with Mother as the matron. To have her and my sisters around was enough security for me, particularly when a year later – what great joy it was! – our cousin brought three-year-old Huda back from Damascus. It was a very special time; we were all together again.

Backbone discipline

Four years later, I was nine years old. The winter of 1953 was a bleak and very cold one. Snow covered the school grounds up to a metre high. It was very beautiful, but the heating was inadequate and we shivered in our classrooms. I suffered severe hand and feet chilblains during this time. Our breakfast dish during wintertime was a Lebanese dish called *kishk* (Middle Eastern porridge). The ingredients were dried wheat, goat's milk and fatty fried meat. We all had difficulty in swallowing the food because of its foul smell and taste. The redeeming factor in giving us girls *kishk* was that it was a good source of energy and protected us from serious colds.

On one particular morning, a freezing cold, snowy one, my sister and I, among twenty other girl boarders, were sitting at the table having our breakfast. As usual, we were complaining and refusing to eat our *kishk* breakfast. Mother, being the no-nonsense mother and matron that she was, decided to punish us, making an example of us to the other girls:

'Iptissam and Afaf, go outside immediately. Take your *kishk* bowls with you and eat the food that God had given you,' she said sternly.

'It is snowing, Mama,' we pleaded, but she took no notice of our pleading.

'You can only come in when you have eaten it all,' was her only reply.

I burst into tears, and quietly took my *kishk* bowl and went outside with my sister. The snow was falling heavily now on the frozen garden. What a sight: two girls, one nine and the other ten years old. I stood shivering in the freezing cold as my chilblained hands trembled, barely able to hold the bowl. The snow fell heavily now. I was desperately frightened and cried more as the white snow turned our long black hair to white. I lost the feeling in my feet too. More tears ran down my numb, frozen cheeks, mixed with the *kishk* I was eating. These tears came down faster when the day students sniggered as they passed us going into their classes that morning. The teachers felt sorry for us and pleaded with Mother to bring us in from the cold and snow, but to no avail. I stood there and carried on crying, shivering, retching and choking, but I ate my plate of *kishk*. Iptissam didn't though. While Mother's back was turned, she buried the contents of her bowl, tipping it on the snowy ground. There were no tell-tale traces visible, as the white *kishk* blended very nicely with the snow. I am not sure if Mother ever found out or even suspected the burial. I learnt my lesson early, that Mother was to be obeyed without questioning, otherwise there would be harsh consequences to be reckoned with.

Looking back as an adult, I believe that Mother's strict disciplinary attitude stemmed from the harsh conditions she had lived through during the two world wars, when food was scarce. In addition, she had deeply held beliefs about being good stewards of what God had given us – so food could never be wasted. Although she was a very strict matron and mother, I accepted it from her because I knew she loved us and was devoted to us.

Two miles outside Baalbeck was the French army barracks, Wavell. After the Second World War, the French vacated it and around nine thousand Palestinian refugees occupied it. UNRWA (United Nations Relief and Works Agency) took over the running of the camp and provided essential services to the refugees in the area. As registered refugees in Baalbeck, we were entitled to the monthly rations. Once a month, a family member had to go to the camp to collect them. One day it was my turn, so I accompanied Warde to the camp to collect them. Warde was the school's Palestinian Muslim refugee cleaner and lived with her family in the camp.

We set out early before the sun got too hot in the sky. I walked and ran breathlessly beside Warde along dusty and dirty roads, passing on our left the massive monolith landmark, Hajar el Hibla ('Stone of the Pregnant Woman' in Arabic). It is more than twenty metres long and, weighing more than 1,100 tons, it was left behind, never reaching its destination when the Romans built the Temple of Jupiter.

Soon Warde and I arrived at the sprawling twelve-building barracks. As I looked, I saw in the distance men and women dressed in long, colourful Palestinian clothes standing in lines, queuing in the dusty parade grounds. Many children were running around and it seemed the whole population of the refugee camp was out.

'Why is everyone standing in line?' I asked Warde.

'Oh,' she said, 'Tuesday is the day when rations are distributed and given out to all the camp's families – they are waiting to collect theirs.'

She gave me my card and said:

'Go and stand in line.'

For two hours I stood there; the sun was getting hotter and hotter, and I was very tired. The noise was deafening – people shouting, children screaming, running around, weaving their way among the queuing adults. At least *they* were enjoying themselves! Fascinated by their play, I wished I were free to join in.

Somewhere in the front of the crowds, a man held a cone to his face and shouted out names. Each time he shouted, someone moved out of the human column and stepped forward.

'Wadia Musallam,' the man shouted through his cone.

Warde, who had joined me, took my hand and pushed me forward. Eventually we reached the man with the loud voice, standing behind a small table. I gave him Mother's ration card, he looked fleetingly down at me, fumbled through the papers in front of him and found Mother's name. He took my index finger, quickly pressed it onto a black ink pad on the table, then stamped my finger on the register, which hurt. I was too young to sign, and most of the refugees did not read or write anyway. This was the proof of our existence, a fingerprint signature – it defined us as refugees. He picked up another stamp and stamped my orange card. When all the stamping was finished, another man handed me a box full of rations: essential provisions of flour, dried milk, oil, soap and tinned food, to last us for a whole month. But on this occasion, Mother asked me to leave our ration box with Warde and her family, as her needs were greater than ours.

Although we did not live in the camp, and had adequate shelter and food at the school, Mother found out that if we did not register each month, our names would be struck off the register, and UNRWA would

21

not pay our school fees. Being refugees, we would not be eligible for any government school funding that existed in those days.

Mother's prime and only interest at this stage was to provide us with the best available education on offer. No doubt, that was at the British school. As far as Mother was concerned, it was acceptable to be without an identity and without money, but not to be without an education. She was adamant that her four girls were going to get the best education available, come what may.

Before we returned to the school, Warde took me to visit her family in the camp. It was a huge structure of a building whose previous occupants were hundreds of French army soldiers. But now, it housed Palestinian refugees instead. As I entered, and wherever I looked, I was confronted by dark walls. I stood in awe as I realised that these walls were not made of brick, but partitions made of thick black jute. Rows and rows of them, hanging from ceiling to floor, forming makeshift rooms measuring only eight by five metres. A curtain-covered opening in the 'wall' formed the entrance door. Each family of up to ten – mother, father, children and grandparents – lived in that one small space. There were many units on each floor, with washrooms and toilets located in separate units outside the main building.

I entered Warde's dark room, rubbing my eyes after being outside in the bright sunlight in order to see clearly. All my senses were assaulted by a combination of smells, sights and noises. When I got accustomed to the small hurricane lamp's flickering light, I saw a room full of shadows, and a delicious spicy smell wafted gently towards me from her kitchen in one corner, that held all her pots, pans and primus stove. A pile of bedding, neatly folded, was on the floor in the other corner. I could not see any chairs or tables anywhere. Instead, cushions were placed in the middle of the floor. Warde pointed to them, so I assumed she wanted me to sit down. I sat cross-legged.

The place was very clean and tidy, but I was disoriented as I heard a lot of loud voices. Nobody was in the 'room' except the two of us, and neither of us was speaking at all. Warde noticed my confusion.

'My neighbours talk very loudly behind the wall,' she explained.

I put our ration box in Warde's kitchen area. She was very pleased to show me off to her neighbours and family: a visitor from the British school where she worked had come to visit her. She offered me sweet tea in a small, golden-decorated glass, and as I drank, a warm glow filled me.

I was happy and proud that I belonged to a school where the teachers and missionaries were very much appreciated and respected.

The school was situated on the main street in Baalbeck, and opposite, facing it, was the only cinema. All during the day and well into the night, loudspeakers would blare Arabic music and songs. I was curious, wanting to explore what went on outside the protective school walls. So whenever I could, I stood just outside the school's big green gate watching passers-by go about their business. In doing so, I of course heard them talking, swearing and cursing in loud voices.

One night after a spell on the street outside, I went to bed but could not sleep as swear words kept coming out of my mouth. I couldn't stop them, so I went sobbing and frightened downstairs to Mother. When she extracted the source of my distress, she got a bowl of soapy water and washed my mouth and sent me back to bed. You see, I was very frightened to upset Mother and God, as Mother had always told us that swearing was wrong and God did not want his name to be used in a bad way. I never had recurring swearing bouts after that.

Many times at night, tucked in bed, I could hear the voices of the camel-men forcing their camels to sit down by the trapdoor on the granary roof, which was located just outside my bedroom windows. In response, the camels moaned and groaned very loudly, showing their displeasure, but sat down eventually, chewing on the cud, while the men unloaded the wheat bales through the trap doors, laughing and shouting. These nightly voices and noises haunted my young mind.

One Sunday during April of 1953, there was a lot of excitement and anticipation as Mother announced that Uncle Naim, the youngest of her seven brothers, was coming to visit us. The last time we had seen him was in Haifa, six years ago. He came and we spent great few days with him. Before he left, he gave each of us girls a five-*piastre* coin (a penny). I was eleven years old and had never been given any pocket money before.

The lost coin

I was so excited and felt very, very rich. I could buy whatever I wanted! Fearing I might lose my shiny new coin, I held it tightly in my hand at all times. Every now and then I checked it was still there by sniffing, touching and looking at it.

The choice of what to buy was confusing: sweets, pens, or maybe I would go to the small shop across the road and look at what they had before I made my decision. My treasure was safe in my hand for days – until one afternoon I stood with my sisters, playing by the green wooden stairs that led up to the flat roof. I was playing with my coin on the railings, when suddenly my precious piece fell in the open slot between the joints – where the railing met the post. It disappeared so quickly! I panicked, but told no one. Later, and on my own, I got a long, thin piece of wood and tried long and hard to dislodge and retrieve it. Tragically, the more I moved it, the more it entombed itself in the slot, a prisoner of two nails. I was devastated at losing my precious coin. For months afterwards, whenever I passed the stairs – and it was many times – I cast a longing, sad eye into the slot to see if my five-*piastre* coin was still there. Yes, it was still there alright. But alas, there was no way of getting it out; and as time – days and months – passed, the coin was eaten up by rust and became less and less visible to the eye. I never mentioned it to anyone, lest I would be told off for being careless in looking after my coin.

I loved the summer holidays. Students, both day and boarders, went home to their families, and as the school was our home, the whole place was ours. One day, we sat in the courtyard by the garden pond enjoying lunch. On the table we had dishes of hummus, stuffed vine leaves, flat bread and lots of fruit. We were very conscious of the six giant, twenty-two-metre, towering Roman pillars behind us in the distance. The impressive temple of Jupiter had stood there since 15 BC and was five minutes' walk from the school. As the sun shone brightly on the two-thousand-year-old huge stones shrouding some parts in shade and mystery, we sat enjoying lunch – until my sister, Siham, asked suddenly with a twinkle in her eyes:

'Anyone seen the midday stars?'

'I would like to see them, as I have never seen them before.' I jumped up excitedly.

'No problem, but are you sure you want to see them?' she continued.

'Yes, I am very sure,' I enthused.

Quickly, an old jacket was produced, one of its sleeves held upright like a funnel over my face to help me see the stars clearly. I had no time to focus as a cold deluge of water drenched my face, blinding me. I screamed and jumped up from my seat, while the others laughed their heads off. The midday stars were etched on my memory for a long time to come.

Mother called us one day to her wooden-partitioned bedroom at the end of the dormitory floor. A large trunk was open in the middle and we stood round it admiring the colourful clothes inside.

'Now, girls,' she said, 'these beautiful clothes that you see in front of you were sent from England, by very generous and good people. People we don't even know. They sent them to us, refugees, because they love us.'

When Mother finished her speech, shouts of glee greeted each item as it came out of the trunk. They were beautiful; we had never seen anything like them before. I loved a black jacket and a green pinafore dress, and asked Mother if I could have them. I was so happy when she agreed; the black jacket had stripes of yellow and red on the sleeves and zip-fasteners in front and on the pockets. I kept opening and closing the zips, wondering what to put in the pockets. Now I not only had my school uniform but two pretty outfits to dress up in. In the 1950's, Baalbeck shops did not sell ready-made clothes such as these, only material to buy for dressmaking. This jacket was so pretty and special; it came all the way from faraway England, donated by rich people, and was sent just for me.

We found a stylish grey soft fur coat at the bottom of the trunk. Sadly, it never saw daylight as Mother never wore it. She would say:

'No. No, I can't wear it; it is too classy for me.'

Whenever I made a trip up the attic to check the trunk, I found the fur coat undisturbed, folded back on itself. It never saw the light or kept anyone warm, confined there for the rest of its life. That trunk with clothes, books and games was just one of many we received from England. The generosity of the British people touched me to the core and instilled in me a life-giving lesson.

This same year we celebrated Christmas in Damascus. We travelled the seventy-seven miles by car over dangerous, winding and snow-capped mountain roads, which were the notorious hashish-smuggling corridor between Lebanon and Syria. There was a lot of kissing and hugging when we arrived. What a welcome! It was so special to see uncles, aunts and cousins again. I felt their love, warmth and care for us as we laughed and cried together. Two of my uncles' families lived together in one house. They really knew how to celebrate Christmas, with toys under the Christmas tree, *Jingle Bells* and Frankie Lane's *Jezebel* blaring from the new HMV record-player. I was so happy. The big, brightly decorated Christmas tree stood guard over all the colourful wrapped presents.

Every now and then it blinked its lights at me, inviting me to find a gift with my name on it. Aromatic cooking smells wafted from the kitchen as Mother and aunts prepared Christmas lunch. We sat down for lunch. What a table, with mouth-watering dishes of stuffed chicken with rice, minced meat, almonds and pine nuts! Next came dishes of stuffed vine leaves, aubergines and courgettes. Wine and Arak (anise-flavoured, 40% alcohol) filled the glasses. So much food, a feast with this big happy clan of uncles, aunts and cousins. I could hardly contain my joy and excitement when my aunt retrieved a large box wrapped in red from under the tree and gave it to me on Christmas Eve. I opened it in a great rush and couldn't believe my eyes when I saw four tiny red and white teacups, saucers and a teapot neatly arranged in the box. I loved it! I was overwhelmed by the generosity of Uncle Adib's family. What a wonderful, beautiful gift. At the age of thirteen it was all I understood of Christmas, but later on in life I understood its true meaning.

On Boxing Day, my teenage cousins asked me to join them playing on the street outside the house. I was reluctant at first as I was not sure about roller skating, but I loved outdoor games since I had grown physically stronger and more confident. They encouraged me, insisting that it was great fun, and lent me two of their metal skates with four tiny wheels. I wore them over my shoes, tightening the screws and fastening the straps round my ankles. Gingerly, I stood up, balancing carefully so as not to fall. No problem, I was OK, and we raced each other up and down the wide, quiet street. Occasionally, a *Huntour*, a two-horse-drawn carriage came by, and this is when the fun started...We did not have to wait long before we heard horses trotting towards us. We were ready now, waiting for the carriage to be in the middle of the road opposite us. When it was there, my cousin shouted:

'One... two... three!'

We lunged forward on our skates and grabbed the black canopy at the back. I hung on precariously, my skates barely touching the ground as the *Huntour* sped on. It was exhilarating! A few yards down the road, I heard and felt a sharp crack as the tip of the long whip stung me. Oh no, the carriage driver had seen us! Screaming and laughing, I let go of the carriage when the whip hit me. The long whip succeeded in dislodging us from the carriage, but not from pursuing our crazy game. It was exciting and great fun.

The first step

Something took place when I was thirteen that had a profound impact on my life then and helped shape my life later on.

Once a year, the school celebrated Founders' Day to commemorate and thank God for the school. That morning was very busy; all the girls cleaned and put flowers in every classroom, which looked really tidy and attractive. Classes were suspended and there was a buzz in the air as we anticipated the afternoon's celebrations.

Pauline, one of the missionaries teaching at the sister school in Beirut, was the main speaker that afternoon. We all gathered in the big hall and listened to her speaking about the second coming of Christ. She stated that we would either be taken up to heaven, if we believed in Christ, or we would stay behind for eternal suffering if we did not. Her talk made a deep impression on me and I went to bed that night worried, thinking about what she had said. It marred all the excitement of the day and I could not think of anything else. In the morning, I woke up after this vivid dream: I was with my classmates when the second coming happened; my closest friend, a Muslim girl, was sitting next to me. When I looked around she was gone. She was taken up to heaven, but I was left behind. I was really frightened and disturbed, especially because I was from a Christian family and she was not – so why was I not taken up with my Muslim friend? The dream was very real.

During the next day's meeting, Pauline gave out the invitation to accept Jesus as one's personal Saviour and have the assurance of eternal life. I don't know where the boldness and courage came from, but I put my hand up. I could not explain what happened next as a profound sense of peace and joy, which I certainly did not have before, came over me. Now I remember Pauline with great fondness, as she was the one who helped me first find out who I was, and where I was going to, on my very long journey in this world.

The mission school in Baalbeck had been our secure home and school since we left Haifa in 1948. During those seven years, I completed junior studies in Arabic, my mother tongue. But as English was the main study language in secondary school, I found it very hard at first to study all subjects in English. We had days in school when we would forfeit points if we spoke Arabic, and at the end of the day, we had to redeem the points with extra English homework. During this time, I discovered how much I enjoyed reading, and read any Arabic book that came into my possession. When I had exhausted all the good and bad Arabic books, I had no choice but to read the English ones. The first of these was *The Robe*, by Lloyd C. Douglas. It captured my imagination and emotions, reinforcing my love for reading. The more I read English books, the more my English improved.

I had seven very happy years in our first home, the school. Our refugee family had outgrown the small school in Baalbeck and now we needed to join secondary classes. The Lebanon Evangelical School for Girls (LESG) in Beirut was the perfect choice as it was the Mission's main school. Also, my eldest sister was already studying there. So in 1955 we moved to Beirut with our few belongings, including Mother's precious farewell gift, a brand new, sparkling, state-of-the-art pressure cooker.

Uncle Halim was a real rock and support to Mother during this time, as he helped us find an apartment near the school and paid the first six months' rent. I shall never forget his care, love and generosity towards us. He was a father figure, replacing the one I never knew.

The new school and the big city were fascinating to me, but I felt completely lost at first. I had gone from the security of a small boarding school to a proper big school; from a small institution to a home environment.

Our new home was a one-bedroom, very small, third-floor match-box apartment. The three younger sisters shared the one bedroom, while Mother and my older sister had the sitting / dining room as their bedroom at night. My grandmother was allowed to leave Haifa and come to Beirut, so it was agreed by all her seven sons that it would be best for her to live with her daughter, i.e. with us. Grandmother had the third room in the house, which was supposed to be a dining room. I recall sitting on her bed many times watching her weave dried palm leaves into the most beautiful, colourful mats.

I will never forget the day the minor earthquake of 1957 struck. Grandmother was the first one out of the flat, hobbling down the stairs – an eighty-year-old, muttering under her breath:

'I don't want to die under the rubble, I don't want to die under the rubble...'

When she joined us from Haifa, she managed to bring out with her our old Singer sewing machine and our birth certificates, which she had picked up from the street where the Jewish family now occupying our home had thrown them. Recovering my birth certificate had a special significance in my life later on.

Beirut was a very sophisticated city and it was expensive to live there. Six of us were cramped into our small apartment. Our living situation became dire as, month after month, money shortages became the norm. Mother tried desperately to find a job but was unsuccessful. One morning, the first day at school, I proudly wore my new school uniform ready to set out. But before we left the apartment, Mother got us together in the small sitting room and prayed that God would find her a job.

After our prayers, the three of us, together with my teacher sister, trooped off to our new school which was seven minutes away. Happy, excited and apprehensive, I looked up and saw Mother on the third-floor balcony, proudly waving us goodbye as we disappeared round the corner. She went back into the flat to finish her chores, but shortly afterwards the doorbell rang. David, the head of the British Syrian Mission in Lebanon, was at the door, so she invited him in. The purpose of his visit was to ask Mother if she would teach the American and English missionaries in Beirut Arabic. Mother had just prayed for a job, hadn't she? There was her answer! She was taken aback, as she was a midwife / nurse, not a teacher. *Of course* she was willing to try. David assured her that all the Arabic phonetic books she needed were available to her. She accepted his offer on the spot, and for the next seven years the family income was secured. For the second time in my life, I could not deny God answering Mother's prayers immediately and in such a dramatic way. The first such answer was when he had answered her prayers in regards to finding the school in Baalbeck and providing transportation leaving Amman. I stored these incidents in my mind.

All foreign and private schools in Beirut were fee-paying. The Lebanon Evangelical School for Girls was a very well known, private and prestigious school and only well-off families were able to send their children there. We were poor, but somehow Mother was able to pay the fees in instalments. In due course, all four of us attended and graduated from the school. I shall never forget the generosity of Freda Button, the headmistress, or my gratitude to her, for paying my school fees one year.

I was secure and settled during all my high school years at the English missionary-run school. I did quite well in my studies and was popular, managing to be the class prefect, basketball captain and school prefect. I took pride in my achievements, and to prove it I had an array of colourful badges attached to my uniform pocket. I loved, and was especially good at, sports. After our class won the schools' basketball trophy one year, one of the teachers said to Mother that she should send me to England to pursue a sporting career. That was pie in the sky, as it would not put food on our plates! Instead, and besides going to school, I worked to contribute to the finances of the family. One of our neighbours, a Muslim family with four children aged between six and twelve, asked Mother if I could oversee their children's studies and homework. I went round every day after school to their house, sat with them and helped them with their Arabic, English and Koran studies. Then I came back home and did my own homework. That was the first time I had set eyes on the Koran, let alone read it. These children, though, were expected both to read and to memorise it.

By this time my reputation for teaching had grown! The worst job I had during these years was teaching a teenager extra Arabic grammar lessons to enable him to pass the government exams. Now, Arabic grammar is a difficult and complicated subject at the best of times. It was a nightmare – but how did I teach something I did not know? I am not sure what I taught him! The problem was that I was timid and did not know how to say no. My dear family expected me to teach, so I did, as I could not let them down.

Besides school, our lives revolved round our church assembly in Beirut. The Brethren church in Haifa, Palestine, under the leadership of Roy Whitman, fled to Amman, Jordan in 1948. Among them was Mother's cousin Munir and his family. Later on they moved to Beirut, Lebanon where they established the Brethren assembly in 1950, which is still going strong today. Many Christian Palestinian refugee families joined this assembly, among them Mother. We regularly attended these meetings, although we were still registered as Anglicans since the Lebanese state did not recognise the Brethren assembly as a church.

The assembly was very strict in its Brethren teachings concerning Christian beliefs and behaviour in a Muslim environment. It instilled in us, from an early age, conservative attitudes in regard to dress and social life. The 'no' list stretched long: no sleeveless dresses, no lipstick or make-up, no jewellery, no swimming, no cinema and very strict conduct between the sexes. This applied to the extent that in church men and women occupied different sections – husband and wife did not sit together. I remember going up the narrow stairs that led to the large hall and meeting boys on the way; I would look the other way, avoiding looking at them, let alone talking to them. The most uncomfortable thing, as far as I was concerned, was the wearing of a scarf during the service, following biblical teaching in 1 Corinthians 11 that women should cover their heads in church. The scarf was very uncomfortable round my neck – and besides, I thought it did not enhance my looks. I made sure that mine slipped gradually and often onto my shoulders. This did not miss Mother's watchful eyes, and her quick hands made sure it did not stay there long. If any woman came in without one on, there was an ample supply of scarves at the top of the stairs, dished out generously by the ever-present Aunt Khazneh, Uncle Munir's wife, who made sure that nothing of a woman's beautiful hair was showing.

One of the things I enjoyed was playing the harmonica with my sister, Iptissam, and when I joined the Sunday school team, I introduced these small musical instruments to all the youngsters in my class. We produced good sounds when we all played together. These boys, later on in the 1970s, composed, played and recorded new Arabic Middle Eastern Christian songs, replacing the translated English ones.

Seven years after my Christian experience and conversion in Baalbeck, and to prove that I was committed to my faith, Mother urged me to get baptised. Now in my late teens, I was very reluctant to take that step at first, since I wasn't sure of the implications. I had been baptised as an infant, but it did not comply with our biblical teachings, so Mother insisted, and later I accepted, that I needed to be baptised as an adult. The service was conducted on the shores of the beautiful blue Mediterranean Sea going south towards Tyre and Sidon from Beirut. It was a hot summer day along a quiet sandy beach, the whole church assembled at the edge of the water. I stood in my long white dress, conscious of how I looked and apprehensive of the coming ceremony. I joined the other women who were taking this step too. One after another they went forward to be baptised. My turn came, and I walked very slowly into the sea, steadying myself as I stepped on the unseen pebbles and looked at the vast blue sea stretching endlessly beyond. The sea was very calm, with hardly a ripple. I kept walking until the water came up to my waist. In front of my pastor and an elder and everyone else, I confirmed my faith. Then they prayed for me and gently helped me under the water. I choked on the salty water when I came out. The congregation welcomed me by singing hymns. Mother met me and was quick in putting a towel over me. In hindsight, although I was hesitant in taking the step, I am glad I took it then, as it was the second step of faith on my long and hard journey. I knew that I was on the right road to find who I was and to be at peace.

In due course, the family moved from the small, crammed apartment to a two-bedroom bigger house with a small garden, that a missionary couple vacated. We were blessed to have this house, as Beirut was a jungle of apartment blocks, and houses with gardens were very rare.

So now, and for the first ten years in Lebanon, we were known as Palestinian refugees. Slowly, things started to improve. We had a comfortable home and attended a good British school. Meanwhile, Mother had established herself as an excellent Arabic teacher to missionaries.

The most dramatic change to our circumstances came during this time. This was thanks to Lebanon's Christian Maronite President at the time, who was desperate to bolster the Christian voting register against the Muslim one. To do so, he issued a presidential decree granting the coveted Lebanese citizenship to around three thousand Christian Palestinian refugee families. We were one of these families. Nearly all details pertaining to our family origins were correct on the forms: I was born in Haifa, Palestine and so were all my sisters. However, it was recorded on my mother's application that she had been born in Zahle, Lebanon instead of in Shefa Amer near Nazareth in Palestine.

Everything in Lebanon had its price: it was expensive to get the citizenship that we were offered, and it took us some years to repay my uncle, who paid the fee up front on our behalf. Gaining Lebanese nationality gave us all a sense of belonging, but it did not help much in altering my accent from Palestinian to Lebanese! With the lack of a genuine Lebanese accent, I had to settle for a mixture of both. From the time I became a national, I believed that I belonged and was a Lebanese citizen. After so many years as a refugee, in the absence of a Palestinian identity, my new sense of citizenship grounded me and gave me a sense of hope and a future.

Lebanon's woes and unrest started in that same year, 1958. Politically, the country was sliding slowly but dangerously into the first signs of sectarian conflict. A Maronite Christian minority population was wielding most governmental powers over the Muslim majority. One night in May, I woke up to loud, chilling screams coming from the modern three-storey building across the road. Immediately, the doorbell rang non-stop. Mother jumped up from her sofa bed in the sitting room and opened the door. I heard loud voices. Mother quickly put on her coat over her night-dress and was gone with whoever was at the door. An hour later she returned.

'I had to look after the men's injuries – they were beaten badly,' she said sadly.

Was history repeating itself? Time had not yet healed our memories. We had not forgotten the fighting in Haifa in 1948, when we had to flee our homes and become refugees. But this was peaceful Lebanon! We were facing another round of danger, fear, anxiety and uncertainty in our new homeland as Muslims and Christians fought each other.

The school year was cut short. For six months in 1958 we were confined to the house and off school as fighting spread around us. I was sad and frustrated, as I loved school and missed my friends. These were the first seeds of discontent and a taster of the vicious civil war that would engulf the country twenty years later.

During this time, a ray of joy penetrated our gloom. One morning, with my sisters, I stood on the veranda overlooking the small garden. We noticed a shivering, tied-up black bundle in the corner, looking pitifully at us.

'A black goat?' we screamed.

'No, a black puppy!' we squealed again with joy.

Delighted with our first pet, we quickly untied him, gave him some milk and named him Blackie.

What was the story of this poor dog, tied up and thrown so cruelly over our garden wall? In the West, children are given puppies for Christmas or birthdays, but not in West Beirut where we lived. There a dog is the lowest of the low, and if you call someone a 'dog', you insult him. Our area was a Muslim neighbourhood, and during the day we had heard the local children parading this small black dog, chanting the Christian President wife's name. Once it was dark, they threw the frightened puppy into the Christian family's garden.

We had hilarious times playing with Blackie during this time confined at home with all schools closed. Once, he reduced us to jittery girls standing on the dining room table screaming as he chased a mouse round the room. He was our playmate and joy for many years to come.

Security in Caracole Druz, where we lived, was getting worse by the day. Mother was very worried about our safety, so she sent us to stay with my uncle's family in the relatively peaceful Hamra district. Things did not go according to her plan, as we started wanting and copying what our cousins did: 'worldly things', according to Mother, like going to the cinema or to the beach. How I loved swimming with my cousins! But these things were not approved by our good Brethren church. Fearing that our Christian witness would be compromised by the way we lived, she recalled us back to Caracole Druz, even though fighting was still going on. I was so sad that our emancipation was short-lived!

I was delighted, though, when life returned to normal after six months of civil disruption and we were able to return to school. Those years were good. I loved the challenge of studying and doing well in sports, wanting to succeed and prove myself in everything. Generally, I did achieve good marks in all my subjects, though I would have had top grades if I had concentrated more on my studies rather than sports and friends. Parents were responsible for their children's education, not the State, so I needed to help financially if I was to continue my schooling. Scholarships were available to both very bright and very needy pupils. Our financial situation and my attainments both fell short of the requirements, so I had to earn some money.

To this end, and through a family friend's recommendation, I went to live as an au-pair with a couple with two children during the summer holidays. In those days, being an au pair was not that common, and Middle Eastern culture did not look favourably on any kind of domestic help. I don't recall if I was asked if I wanted to go, but I do remember that I was expected to! Even if it was not what I wanted to do, I had the example of a selfless, giving Mother, plus an older sister who was a teacher, working hard and contributing to the family finances. My younger sister was too young to go. That left Iptissam, who was one year older than me, but she did not want to go, so off I went to one of Lebanon's most beautiful mountain villages, Beit Mery, where this family lived. Their wealth manifested itself in their smart, luxurious house as well as their fruit orchards.

My job was to look after the children during the day, either by helping them with their summer school homework or by organising their play time. It seemed to me that my job was to entertain them so that their mother could entertain her friends! I was young and inexperienced, especially in looking after school-age children. Perhaps this job affected me negatively, as later on I did not choose to become a teacher, which was one of the most common vocations for women in those days. The only good thing was that my earnings helped pay my school fees.

Many times during the day, I would pass through their very expensively furnished but hardly used dining room. In the middle stood a large mahogany table with a big fruit bowl on it. Next to it there was always a silver plate full of *baklava*, a Lebanese sweet kind of puff pastry, and pistachios. *Baklava* was a very expensive dessert, which I longed for but had hardly had the chance to eat when I was young. There was so much of it in front of me all the time that the temptation was too great to resist. One day I could not stop myself, and I picked up one or two pieces. It was delicious, but my Christian conscience reminded me that I had stolen that which did not belong to me. I had been too embarrassed to ask if I could have one.

My last day in high school came on 30th June 1960. I was eighteen – what excitement! I had passed all my school exams plus GCE History and Geography. On that Graduation Day, all the girls wore white dresses with high heels – they were my first – and paraded down the steps into the graduation venue, the school's playground, where the ceremony took place. Mother, my sisters, and all my relatives and friends assembled. I was a proud graduate when I received my high school certificate and a small financial prize.

Everyone, including me, expected me to continue my studies at the university. Alas, my grades were not up to the mark. I qualified to receive a scholarship from UNRWA only if I achieved 80+ averages – I got 78. I had given friends, sports and the Top Twenty music chart a larger portion of my study time and it was an expensive mistake.

However, soon afterwards I was presented with an exciting alternative:

'How would you like to go to the States?' asked Miss Mi'mary, a teacher at the school and a family friend. 'You might like to become an X-ray technician in Tampa, Florida.'

I was excited at the prospect of adventure and training, and succeeded in securing a place at the X-ray department at the main hospital in Tampa. My life was about to begin, but how was I to leave the family? I was apprehensive and excited at the same time, dreaming what life had in store for me. Full of anticipation, I went to the USA embassy to get my visa… My application was refused. Maybe they questioned my reason for going to the States. They were not completely wrong, as Miss Mi'mary had lined me up to marry a much older relative of hers when I got there. I was devastated. In one year I had experienced two major disappointments. My faith was dormant at this stage, waiting in the background, but I was determined that I would not let circumstances affect believing in myself and trusting in what I could achieve.

Work and college

Every Palestinian family's dream was to give their children the best education to see them through life. With no homeland to call their own, security, roots or identity, all parents knew that education would give the next generation a tangible arm to reach the unreachable. I too realised that without higher education, I would not be able to achieve much, and felt that I had let myself and everyone else down. Instead of going to university, I enrolled in a shorthand / typing course at a YWCA venue. What a climb down! However, through cousin Afaf's high Middle East Airline contacts, nine months later I landed a good secretarial job with a well-known investment company. This company and its directors were to play a very special part in my future.

My mother was very proud of me, and so was I. I felt I was climbing the Lebanese social ladder, shedding off my refugee status. Secure in my social standing, surrounded by strong, supportive family members and many friends, I felt at home in my adoptive country. An observant person would have noticed the slight variation in my pronunciation and concluded that I was a Palestinian. But with the Lebanese nationality in my pocket, the feeling of belonging was cemented. Our family had embraced the Lebanese culture and society, both Christian and Muslim. As far as I was concerned, I was a happy and proud Lebanese.

My pride and joy

To crown my status, my generous brother-in-law, Scott, gifted me with a brand-new Morris car. In a small country like Lebanon, with a population of two million in the 1970s, appearances were all that mattered. So if you had a car, your status shot up accordingly. In my eyes, I was at the top of the ladder. The Morris car dealership was owned by the company I worked for, and as a goodwill gesture to the director's secretary, LP 1,000 was taken off the LP 5,000 retail price. To own a brand-new car really bolstered my confidence and enhanced my self-assurance. I felt such exhilaration and freedom the first time I took it out on my own as a licensed driver.

These two acts of generosity helped towards building up my faith in God, although I was still a novice in trusting Him completely for my needs.

To be a licensed driver in Beirut in those days, one had to pass a driving test on a long stretch of empty road. I had to put the car in the required gear, do a three-point turn, drive along and park. Alas! That did not prepare me for driving on the fast, crazy-busy Beirut streets. In a recent survey, Beirut topped the twenty most dangerous cities to drive in. At that time, driving safely was non-existent, and driving codes were little known, acknowledged or respected. (Sadly, today the situation is even worse.) So to acquire the needed confidence and ability to drive on the chaotic, dangerous Beirut streets and stay alive, after I had passed my test, I booked lessons with a private driving instructor.

I chose a quiet Sunday afternoon for my practice run, when roads were less busy. But before my instructor arrived, an impulse took hold of me.

'I am taking the car round the block,' I shouted to Mother.

'Can't you wait for the instructor to come?' she replied.

But by then, I was halfway down the lift to the garage. My heart was pounding fast; I could hear it as I got in the new car. I was so apprehensive that I did not even notice the smell of the new, bright green leather of the interior. My hand shook so much that I fumbled to turn on the ignition. Still shaking uncontrollably, I put the car in first gear and rolled out onto the street. After one kilometre round the block, I was still in first gear and was the only car on the road. I reached the junction, nine hundred metres from home, and turned left. Seconds later, I heard a mighty bang and the car was facing a concrete wall! I was in shock as I realised what had happened: a speeding car had crossed the junction on my right. I had kept going and the other driver had not stopped, shunting my car until the wall stopped it. I sat shivering and shaking, looking at the damaged front of the new car. Gingerly I opened the jammed door and extracted myself from behind the wheel. That was when I noticed that my elbows were bleeding and bruised. I stood on wobbly legs at a loss what to do next, when who should pass at that precise moment but my driving instructor, coming to collect me for my practice run.

'What have you done!?' was his only remark.

I kept quiet but I thanked God that I did not have any broken bones and also that the Kurdish children, who usually played at this corner during the week, were not there that Sunday. The instructor towed the car to a garage, while I went home and nursed my pride and injuries.

Outwardly, I appeared to everyone to be a confident, capable person. Mother looked up to me. Wasn't I the breadwinner at home? I had a good job with status and now a new car. But on the inside, something was still missing, and I knew it. The disappointment I felt by not getting into university weighed heavily on me. I was determined to do everything in my power to achieve the missing link in my life – get a degree. But how was I going to achieve this while working full time?

The ultimate goal

The answer came when Haigazian College, one of the new colleges in Beirut, started evening classes. I was one of the first students to enrol on the Business Administration programme, with English as the study language for all courses except the Arabic ones. The American study system was made up of credits – taking forty courses, with three or four credits each, would give me a BA degree. Here was the chance to earn my living during the day and study to achieve my goal. From 9 am to 5 pm, I sat behind my personal-assistant desk in an investment company, and when 6 pm came, I collected my books and went and sat in a college classroom till 10 pm.

After two years of this heavy schedule, taking three courses a term, I discovered that the evening class syllabus was not offering the courses I required to complete my degree. I was resigned to this disappointment, but my boss was not; he was aware of my situation and knew how much I wanted to pursue my studies. He called me into his office before the new term started and offered to pay all my course fees, both the ones I had already paid for and the new ones I needed to take. He said, reassuring me:

'Afaf, this is not a loan, as long as you pursue the BA programme. Also, I would like to authorise job-day-release for you so that you can attend daytime classes but remain on full salary.'

I was overjoyed and thanked him for his generosity.

What a great turn of events! Wasn't that my goal and ambition? Could I have planned it better myself? I doubt it very much; the Master Planner was in control of all these events.

For five years afterwards, I managed to follow this concentrated schedule of work during the day and attend classes in the evenings. Unfortunately, I could not sustain the rigorous pressure I put myself under. So in 1971, I left the programme without taking the last two courses I needed for my final six credits. It was a big disappointment, but something positive came out of all this. I was offered the chance to train as an assistant accountant, with a view to gradually taking on more of the company's accounting procedures and responsibilities. I was thrilled to start climbing the professional ladder.

I was now at an age where young women of my generation dreamt of getting married, and I was no different, especially as my three sisters were already married. Their marriages were not typical Middle Eastern ones, where two people meet through family contacts. Siham met Ron, who was British, during a visit to London arranged by the British Council. They married in Beirut and moved to England to live. Iptissam met Scott, an American, at a church choir practice. They married in Beirut and went to live in the States. Huda met Ramsis, who was Egyptian, at a Christian youth conference. They married in Beirut and ended up in the States too. On many occasions, I wondered whom I would marry and where I would end up. I worried a lot, knowing that in Middle Eastern culture if a girl did not marry, she would end up living with the family until her dying days. Would that happen to me?

Some years earlier when I was eighteen, I had spent a summer at a Christian conference centre in the mountains of Lebanon, Dhour Chweir, and worked as a waitress. It was hard work and long hours. While I was there, I was overcome by a strange feeling, never felt before – you know, the fluttering one – after I was introduced to a tall, handsome young man. Was it love at first sight or just my first crush? I wasn't sure. Unfortunately for me, he was oblivious of my existence! Being so bashful and introverted meant that nobody guessed my feelings, including him. I kept them to myself, especially when I learnt that he was looking for a wife Middle Eastern style, where the family go searching for a suitable wife among friends. I knew I was no match compared to the beautiful accomplished young woman he was introduced to. So ultimately my feelings never saw daylight, as I buried them for good.

In my early twenties and during my college evening study, I got to know a very kind and generous man in the same class. Every evening he would pick me up from home and drive me back when the session ended. We became good friends and he even took me and introduced me to his family, who lived in a beautiful village in the Chouf Mountains. There was, though, a big barrier to our having any future together. In our church, any young man outside our small Brethren circle of believers was not an acceptable addition to the family. My friend was not a Christian but belonged to the Druze religion, an offshoot of Islam. Moreover, I was so occupied with my studies and work that this episode disappeared from my life with no lasting damage to my emotions.

The inevitable Middle Eastern style marriage introductions and proposals were also available during the same period. Our Brethren church was very strict in matters of relationships and who got to know whom. With limited and restricted face-to-face interaction, it was very hard to get to know any young men in our church. Our minister's wife was the marriage broker, and in that capacity she arranged for one of the eligible young men and me to meet. The passage of time has erased his name from my memory, but I recall he was from the northern town of Zahleh. I agreed to meet him, convincing myself that this was not an arranged marriage proposal, which I detested the thought of.

'If you agree to meet him, that means you will marry him,' the minister's wife informed me.

'But how can I do that? I hardly know the man. Give us a chance to get to know each other first,' I pleaded.

She stuck to her requirements and I stuck to mine. The young man and I never met nor got married! Middle Eastern society was changing, and young women in my generation had adopted a more progressive outlook. I was flattered that someone had noticed me and wanted to marry me, but surely I had a choice in the matter too.

Next on the proposal-arranged-marriage list, I was introduced to a distant relative in the States. The verbal 'engagement agreement' was by phone and I had never set eyes on him. I only received an old passport-size photo depicting a handsome young man with green eyes of maybe twenty years old, and not the thirty-year-old that I was told he was.

I was excited at the prospect of a new life and new future to look forward to, a new man to share my life with, a new place to go to away from my confined and restricted environment. At last, I would follow my sisters and live abroad. But sadly, as the remote engagement procedures piled on, my excitement dwindled, and doubts and uncertainty crept into my mind and emotions.

What am I doing? I questioned myself. *I haven't met the man in person. What would happen if I went to the States to get married, met him for the first time and realised that I had made a big mistake? It would be too late then, wouldn't it?*

These thoughts and his nightly phone calls disturbed my peace.

There was another big factor that contributed to my doubts. Had I forgotten Mother's very unhappy marriage? Her disastrous arranged marriage to my father when she cared for someone else? What she went through, both before and during the refugee years? Didn't I say I would never agree to an arranged marriage? How could I forget all the distress, upheaval and sadness of these years? My thoughts frightened me. I did not want to end up like Mother, stuck in a loveless, unhappy arranged marriage.

I could not turn away from facing the two persisting big questions: Did I want to stay single all my life? Or alternatively, did I want to risk a burdened, unhappy and miserable marriage?

Added to all this doubt and confusion, I was longing to be free from Beirut's restrictive and suffocating atmosphere. Mother and I were living together, but I don't think that she ever understood my situation or that I appreciated all her sacrifices and struggles in bringing us up. I was struggling emotionally, getting used to being the only daughter still at home; the laughter and chatter that filled our home disappeared when the three sisters married and left. They and their support were far away. I did not realise it then, but I was coming to terms with responsibility for Mother; she did not have any income of her own, so I had to look after her in the absence of a social security system to do so.

Another problem I was facing was that I was now in my thirties, an undesirable marriage threshold in Middle Eastern society, and my 'prince charming' had not yet appeared. I was in a dilemma, unhappy, anxious and confused, knowing full well that I might not have a better chance than the distant relative's proposal. Again and again, I weighed and rationalised all the arguments that were in front of me. The conclusion I reached, after a distressing time, was that although this was a kind of arranged marriage, it was the best way forward at the time. That was why I agreed to get 'engaged'. However, during these long 'engaged' months, the distress and the burden of disagreeing on where to get married – in Beirut or in the States – convinced me that there was no future in this union. I ended it with the sense of a burden lifting from my shoulders.

4

Civil War

Lebanon – 1975

O ver the past twelve years, Antoine, Mary and I had forged a good friendship. With the help and guidance of Middle Eastern InterVarsity Fellowship's British leaders, we were able to establish the Lebanon InterVarsity Fellowship, LIVF, a Christian organisation among university students. The aim was to strengthen and help them to study the Bible by belonging to study-groups during their student years.

Up to 1975, I was working full time during the day, studying at night college and still had time to be completely involved with LIVF. I was very busy, but quite comfortable and fulfilled. I had a well-paid job that enabled me and my friends to visit places like Petra in Jordan, Damascus in Syria and Cairo in Egypt. I also had the opportunity to visit one sister twice in the UK, another sister once in Switzerland, and went on a business trip to a sister company there. It was also such a blessing to attend an InterVarsity student conference at the beautiful Schloss Mittersill in Austria. In my mid-thirties, life was great.

So was Lebanon. It was a thriving country, called the Switzerland of the Middle East. Trade and tourism flourished, with luxurious hotels and villas dotting Beirut's coastal strip, as well as the beautiful mountains of Lebanon. This boom helped to accommodate the influx of people from the surrounding hot countries. They came with their big families, big cars and fat wallets; fleeing the suffocating, stifling heat of the Gulf, exchanging it for the beautiful cool and refreshing climate of the mountain villages and towns.

Unforgettable scent of pine,
Golden gorse and warm wild thyme.
Deep blue calm of the summer seas,
Deep green shade of the cedar trees,

Tinkling bells in the evening glow,
Twinkling lights on the plain below,
Hermon pink in the sunset light,
Baalbek's splendour that age defies–

Gifts from the land of Lebanon.[1]

But alas, this same year saw the seed of discontent raise its ugly head among the two and a half million inhabitants. There were around 200,000 mostly Muslim Palestinian refugees in the camps. The rest of the population was divided along ethnic and religious affiliations. The last census was conducted in 1932 by the French. Eleven years later, in 1943, at the end of the Mandate, the French gave Lebanon its Independence. The Lebanese republic was born with a national unity government formed. The presidency and army generals' positions were given to the Christian Maronites. The Muslims, Sunni, Shiite and Druze, an offshoot of Islam, were given lower positions in the government and army. A power-sharing sectarian system was established.

Thirty-two years later, in 1975, the demographic population distribution had shifted clearly towards a majority Muslim population. They demanded equality and a fairer representation in government. While vigorously voicing their dissatisfaction with the sectarian government structure, they insisted that a census was needed to confirm their claim. In the midst of all this confusion, the stability of the country was threatened by the presence of the armed Palestinian refugees in the camps. The discontent was also fuelled by the big social divide and the lack of national identity. No question, the composition of the country had religious, social and political divisions entrenched in its fabric. It seemed that after all these years of independence, Lebanese nationalism was still in its infancy, unable to unite the country under its flag. The country was divided into factions: the people's first allegiance was to their families, then to their religious affiliations and lastly to their country. Also, we could not ignore the strong interests of neighbouring countries in the affairs of little Lebanon, which added a dangerous and flammable element to this cauldron-mix.

It is a small country, just over ten thousand square kilometres in area, two hundred and ninety kilometres from north to south and a hundred

---

[1] By permission from Brenda DeSmidt – Extracts from a poem written by Hazel St John to Brenda DeSmidt – both lived and worked in Lebanon.

and twenty-nine kilometres across at the widest point. The two hundred thousand refugees shared this tiny place, living in shanty dwellings in four huge camps. Their aid came only from UNRWA. The government did nothing to help them; its only contribution was to keep them stateless. The refugees had no identity whatsoever, except the identity of a stateless human being, which sealed their very marginalised existence. The dream that one day they would go back to their homeland vanished when they ended up in Lebanon after losing their homes in Palestine in 1948.

What ignited the simmering inferno?

On Monday, 20th April, I arrived at the office. The minute I got in, I felt the tension: no one was doing any work as they were all discussing the morning news. The atmosphere was charged with fear and anxiety. Colleagues talked about what had happened and it did not take me long to learn the facts. Four days earlier, four Christian Phalanges party members had been killed outside a church, and it was assumed it was the work of Palestinian militia. The revenge attack had taken place that morning: a busload of Palestinian families on a day outing had been ambushed and slaughtered. It was the spark that lit and plunged the country into an open civil war for the next fifteen years. More than two hundred thousand were killed, seventeen thousand 'disappeared' and one million were displaced. Beirut was divided by the so-called Green Line into two: a Christian enclave to the east and a Muslim one to the west. This imaginary Green Line was in fact the main road that passed through the centre of the built-up city. It became the dreaded buffer zone; the guns of the two militias' snipers, hiding in office blocks, would pick off anyone who dared cross it.

Day by day the suffering of the country continued. Added to the destruction from within was the destruction from without. Relentless Israeli jets made incursions into Lebanese airspace, gripping us with fear. Flying low, two sonic booms heralded their presence first as they flew in screaming. The loud hiss came second, followed immediately by the dreaded rattling explosion, which shattered our lives and our peace. It did not matter whether their targets were wealthy high-rise buildings by the seashore, or shanty dwellings in the refugee camps; these airstrikes treated them both the same way. These bombs completely destroyed local buildings, flattening them on top of their residents' heads.

While this was going on, the fiercest fighting was along the Green Line, fifteen minutes' walk from our flat. On any given day, whichever militia was in control of the Green Line military shelled the other side mercilessly. The bombardment of local neighbourhoods continued unabated for weeks on end, day and night. On summer nights, I lay in bed but was unable to sleep in the sweltering heat, wearing ear mufflers to deaden the sounds of exploding bombs. Looking out of the balcony door in my bedroom, I would be mesmerised by the lights of the tracer bullets as they hissed and zigzagged across the darkened skies. One night I held my breath, knowing what was coming, and counted: one, two, three. A muffled thud and a mighty explosion followed that shook the building like a toy. After the first one, the bombs came down so fast I lost count. The pattern repeated itself over and over again: the light, the hiss, the thud, the deafening explosion. Our third-floor apartment trembled like a drunk, its windows and doors shook and rattled. The lull in the fighting came in the morning and only then we were able to sleep.

We thanked God we were still alive when we woke up. Every day was like the day before, checking that family members and friends were well and safe. We would check the buildings in our neighbourhood that had been damaged during the night's aerial bombardment. This time, God had spared our building but not our neighbours'. Recalling those nights, I remember the feelings of dread, danger, fear, anxiety and hopelessness that I lived with.

Despair filled every moment. Our minds were numbed by what was happening, and we could not understand why our beloved carefree Lebanon had ceased to exist. There was a complete destruction of all governmental infrastructures. Public utilities disappeared; the electricity grid and water storage facilities that supplied Beirut were bombed to smithereens. Nights were long, and candlelight did not help to shorten them. We forgot how it felt to turn on a tap and taste a drink of water. To deal with the shortages, those with sufficient funds dug artisan wells on their properties. Uncle Halim, Mother's brother, was one of those conscientious landlords who invested in a well, supplying us with water.

You would be forgiven if you mistook the digger's rattle-tattle noise, digging up the premises in search of water, for that of machine gun fighting outside. The two sounded very similar. Fighting was street to street, quarter to quarter. Indiscriminate artillery bombardment reduced the thriving *souks* (markets) and commercial centres to unrecognisable rubble. Bombed luxury hotels stood guarding the sea with darkened windows, doors and balconies. No weapon was spared: recoilless rifles, hand-held Katyusha rockets, RPGs (rocket-propelled grenades) and anti-tank guns were among the list. But the human cost of the dead and disappeared was more tragic than any material loss in this conflict.

The rubbish and its stench, suffocating us in the summer heat, piled up high in the streets and alleyways of our quarter, Caracole Druz. The neighbourhood militias took it upon themselves to organise themselves into mini 'police' and 'public service' providers. It was a semblance of law and order, enforced by the gun. They made sure that the bakeries that had not been bombed still baked and distributed bread equally among the residents. Our neighbours, the Muslim armed faction, delivered our bread when it was scarce; and, on another occasion, recovered my stolen car radio. We were a Christian family in a Muslim neighbourhood. They respected Mother, who showed them daily Christian love and care, and won their affection in return.

After a few months of complete chaos and anarchy, Lebanon had spiralled into a full-scale civil war that engulfed the whole country. The regular Lebanese army disintegrated, and three militias filled its void: a Christian one, a Muslim one and a Palestinian one. Each took up arms against the others, saying they wanted to protect themselves from the dangers within the country. They also said they wanted to protect their borders from the dangers without, from the south. No town or village was spared, but Beirut took the brunt of it all; the jewel of the Middle East, frequented by many educated, influential people and businesses, it had been the playground for the rich from all over the globe. The onslaught on the commercial and hotel quarter by the sea was the most ferocious, vicious and totally destructive. Old Roman downtown Beirut was completely reduced to rubble.

We found ourselves scanning the newspapers each morning, counting how many people had been killed, kidnapped, assassinated or had disappeared. What roads were open, safe and passable? The outdoor, fun-loving, hospitality-soaked nation found itself imprisoned by fearful anxiety, confined indoors for weeks on end. We could not go out of our flats; if we did, we were gripped by a terror of being shot at or kidnapped. Knitted into this fear was the crippling anxiety of the dark, hopeless and unknown future. To forget our miserable situation, we spent hours playing cards or Scrabble with neighbours in our building. It is amazing how human nature can adapt and adjust to any situation. Our minds programmed our emotions to accept the abnormal chaos and deadly fighting in our streets as a very, very normal situation.

But why would anyone in their right mind take up arms against their neighbours, whom they had lived happily alongside for decades? Why did they do it? It seemed they had lost their minds; they were behaving as if demented.

Their dangerous madness went beyond the daily atrocities they committed. Once they had sent bombs to the other side of the divided city, they would then phone the residents to ask where their bombs had fallen!

Besides accepting the inevitability of our situation, Mother and I, with many of our friends and church family, had an underlying assurance and hope that kept us going. Our faith in God gave us strength to face all our daily challenges. We knew we could trust Him to protect us and keep us safe. We prayed and encouraged each other over the phone (when the phone system functioned). Kidnapping was rife, so when we had to go somewhere, we made sure that both parties, the party we were going to see and the party we left, knew of our safe arrival.

Don't argue with a gun

Life had to go on!

One morning in 1975, during the first month of the civil war, I decided to try to go to the office, as I was still employed. The night had been reasonably quiet, with little shelling and gunfire in the streets. I set out in my green Morris car at 9 am, together with a colleague who lived in the same building block as I did. We travelled in one car for security and safety reasons. I took and followed the safer roads that the morning news bulletin had recommended, as they knew what roads had militia-manned roadblocks or were involved in fighting. We came to the first red traffic light, and I stopped like the law-abiding citizen that I was. This traffic light had not been shot and disabled yet, so I waited patiently for it to turn green.

Immediately, five loud shots rang out behind us. I jumped up in my seat and looked in the back mirror. The car driver behind me was half-way out of his car window, shouting at us and waving his arms in the air. I looked again and saw a small black gun in his hand. In a split second I understood – I was in his way. Intimidated, with frayed nerves, I had one thing on my mind: to get away from danger as fast as I could. I put my foot down on the accelerator and sped on like crazy. Red traffic light or not, no way was I going to argue with his gun.

What was behind that jeep?

Over time the true horror of this nightmare slowly dawned on us: there was no end to this civil war.

Guns in the Middle East had other uses apart from moving on traffic and killing people. Shooting in the air was also done to celebrate weddings, feasts and many other festivals. The more shooting and the louder the noise, the happier people were.

How that was demonstrated one Sunday afternoon – but for all the wrong reasons! It had been a night of fierce shelling between East and West Beirut. The street below our flat, normally so bustling and busy, was eerily quiet that day, and unusually empty of traffic and people. All the shops were closed and we stayed indoors, not daring to go out. It was a spooky kind of stillness, and a sense of fear and foreboding prevailed.

Out of the blue, and shattering the afternoon's unusual silence, I heard muffled shouting and heavy gun fire coming from far down the street. The noise got closer and closer, louder and louder. I was on the balcony in a flash to see what was happening, my heart pounding fast, but I relaxed a little when I heard celebratory gunfire and cheering. A strong gunpowder smell now filled the air. I looked down from the third-floor balcony onto the street below, as firing in the air continued. A machine-gun-mounted jeep sped towards our building, full of jubilant but hysterical men firing their lethal weapons in the air. The jeep passed our building and was now in full view. Hypnotised, I froze, then shook uncontrollably at what I saw being dragged behind the vehicle. I rushed inside, sick to my stomach, as I recognised the grisly sight.

I cried and shivered with fear, whispering, 'Oh Lord, why this atrocity? Why is a headless corpse being dragged in the streets as a trophy?'

The car sped on, the shooting and cheering died down, and a gloomy stillness descended on the empty street, still filled with the smell of gunpowder. I was haunted by this gruesome sight, seared on my mind for a long time to come.

No one knew who the man was or where he came from, and I wondered if his family ever found out what had happened to their father, husband, brother, son or uncle. The man was just one of the disappeared, kidnapped or killed at a roadblock that night. He must have carried the wrong identity card and been in the wrong part of the city. Now he was paraded as a prize of war. In tomorrow's newspapers he would be one of the numbers that had vanished the night before.

How many more met their end that way? No one knew for sure, but thousands on both sides went missing without a trace. Jameel, a schoolteacher I had known, was one of these. A member of our church, very fervent in evangelising the Muslim side, he was missing for a week before they found him on a rubbish heap, murdered.

Where was the sniper?

The War of the Hotels was in full swing at this time. The most luxurious were St George's, Phoenicia and the Holiday Inn hotels – the pride of Beirut and the Middle East. They suffered systematic bombardment by the warring militias that left them gaping toothless at the vast blue ocean in front of them. Most of the time these fierce battles were fought with heavy exchanges of rocket and artillery fire from the various hotel rooftops and rooms, reinforced by sniper fire, leaving the densely populated neighbourhoods traumatised and a living hell.

To escape the drudgery of boredom and to deaden the frightening bombardment explosions coming across from the hotels' area – two miles away from our house – I sat on the settee one day watching the unreal world of *Dallas* on a small black-and-white TV (before the electricity grid was bombed). I just wanted to give my frazzled nerves a respite from the distressing reality of explosions, kidnappings and killing. The settee was five yards away from the open French doors of our rounded third-floor balcony. The real world outside and around me was all destruction and death, but in stark contrast I was watching the fictional lives of the super-rich.

Halfway through the programme, the sporadic street shootings escalated, and merged with the medley of bombs and rockets exploding in the hotel district. I sat there daydreaming, shutting out everything except the extravagant pictures in front of me. Gun shots rang out suddenly and in succession, louder, nearer, and somehow different from all other gun shots I had heard before. I ignored it at first – but wait a minute! What was that dull thud and those tiny white flakes that hit my hair?

Instinctively, I turned my head and looked back at the wall behind me. There, just above my head, I saw a neat, fresh little hole in the white concrete wall. When I realised it was a bullet hole, I jumped up and ran, very scared, towards the kitchen. But before I reached safety, I heard more gun shots, and this time one bullet whizzed past me through two open doors, embedding itself in the kitchen wall.

At the time, with Mother, I pacified my tortured mind, saying to myself, 'Ah well, these were stray bullets from the street below,' and left it at that. But, later on, I thought to myself, *Hold on, it can't be stray bullets! The balcony is at least five metres away from the sofa where I was sitting. If the gun were fired in the air from the street below, surely the bullets would go straight upwards, spend themselves and fall back down to the street... However, instead, these travelled at least thirteen metres up in a straight line, then made a sharp-right-angle detour into our third floor sitting room and kitchen. How could that be? Unless, unless these bullets were... intended for our flat?*

I could not accept the thought that someone – not once but twice – had aimed his gun and shot at us deliberately. Was it someone sixty metres away from us, on the third floor of the opposite building, standing in his sitting room with a gun in his hand? Or was it someone aiming his gun at our flat from the street below?

We knew some of our neighbours, but not all of them. I did not want to acknowledge that the sniper could be living opposite us or was someone I met daily on the street. Our family was one of the few Christian families living in a Muslim neighbourhood, and I was unable to process the complex implications of being shot at by a neighbour. Like frightened ostriches, both Mother and I hid our heads in the sand. The only way we knew how to deal with the situation was to bury our confused fears in the subconscious of our minds, pretending we had been victims of random stray bullets and not a sniper neighbour.

Yet surely Someone somewhere was looking after us. Two bullets and two misses.

Thank you, Lord, for protecting us.

Kidnapped?

During this same year another ceasefire was agreed, leading to a lull in one of the fiercest fighting periods we had yet seen. We knew it would not last long, like so many others before it. So a group of us from the

Lebanon InterVarsity Fellowship took advantage of the temporary inactivity of the guns and accepted Antoine's invitation to his house in the town of Aley, one of the last safe towns situated in the beautiful Chouf mountain area. We had been deprived of these wonderful social visits for so long now that their absence had become the norm. We longed to live normal lives, free of fear, anxiety, depression and danger.

The warring sides may had been busy restocking their arsenals in preparation for the next round, but we threw all fear and anxiety to the wind. We set out in two cars. I was driving a Volkswagen, with Mother next to me. Wendy, a teacher friend from Eastwood College and LIVF member, was driving the other car with Pam, an LIVF staff worker, and a married couple in the back. Mother was not supposed to come with us but had joined us at the last minute when a very frightened friend dropped out from coming. We drove approximately half an hour south following the coastal road until we reached the mountain road, which was narrow, winding and rugged. We arrived in Aley half an hour later, safe and sound.

What a great day we had. What a joy! To be with friends after being cooped up in our apartments for weeks on end. What peace! We heard not one single gunshot or explosion. What a delight to be away from the fearful stifling atmosphere that was Beirut. Aley was a relatively peaceful town at this stage in the civil war, and the short four hours we were there were the best medicine for our tired bodies, souls and minds.

We decided to return at dusk before the roads became dangerously unsafe at night. There were two road choices. We could either return by taking the main safer road into Beirut, or we could take the same route we had come on, by the scenic, narrow, rugged and dangerous road passing through small villages. I wanted to take the safer main road, but was undecided, and at the end I was overruled and we returned by the same scenic route.

Slowly the round orange sun was setting beyond the horizon as we drove down towards Beirut. In front of us, in the distance, we saw the city: at first glance it seemed to be lying peacefully by the blue Mediterranean, but as we looked closer, we saw a hazy umbrella covering it like a halo. Our beloved Beirut was burning, and our hearts bled for our identity and existence. We drove on as we witnessed the last rites of the setting sun. Its burning edges dipped in the vast ocean and lit the shimmering sea with a beautiful orange glow. We hoped against all hope that when it rose again on the morrow, the Lebanese would come to their senses and stop killing each other for the sake of their beautiful land.

I drove very slowly and followed Wendy's car down the winding mountain road. We chatted as we enjoyed the beautiful tinted scenery in front of us, until the sun rays disappeared completely, plunging the rugged countryside into a shadowy dark veneer. Ten minutes into our journey and halfway down the mountain road, I noticed two strange figures standing silently in the middle of the narrow, darkened road.

'Who are these people and what are they doing?' I asked in disbelief

No one answered me while we approached them slowly. As we grew closer, the figures became more distinguishable; two long guns were being aimed at us by two masked men in Kaffiyeh headdresses, who stood straddling and blocking our way.

Wendy's car screeched to a sudden stop and so did mine. I saw two very agitated gunmen approaching Wendy's car, gesticulating and talking in loud voices.

I could not hear clearly what was being said, but in the next minute I saw passports being handed out of the car window – all in Wendy's car were foreign nationals. Then one gunman opened the back door, pulling out the only male passenger. All of a sudden, I saw Wendy and Pam get out and move towards the back.

'The kidnapped and the disappeared' flashed red in my mind. I hadn't forgotten the numbers of those I had read about in the day's morning newspapers. Without uttering a word, I jumped out of the car, with Mother's words ringing in my ears:

'Afaf, whatever are you thinking? Get back inside.'

Cautiously but firmly, I approached the other car as one of the masked men was sliding behind the wheel.

'What are you doing and what do you want?' I blurted out and demanded hoarsely in Arabic. I did not recognise my voice; it was so unfamiliar, strong and very authoritative.

Two pairs of hardened young eyes peered out at me from behind their Kaffiyehs. They could only had been sixteen or seventeen years old. 'The army is chasing us and we want to get to the coastal road out of their reach,' they stated quickly in Arabic. My mind was racing now.

'I'll take you there; come with me,' I demanded breathlessly.

Without another word said, they walked with me to my Volkswagen. I asked my two friends in the back to get out, then quickly but gently helped in the two lads and their heavy guns. I closed the door, got behind the wheel next to my mother, fumbled with the ignition and drove off nervously. They were silent and no one said a word. Then, one mile down the road...

'STOP, STOP!' they screamed in high pitched voices.

I slammed my foot on the brake and the car shuddered and stopped. Immediately, another gunman ran out from the bushes and got in. There were three guns now in the small car; one rested heavily on my shoulder and pointed to the road ahead and the others were aimed at the car's side windows. With fingers ready on the triggers, the gunmen were in a very heightened and agitated state, now talking loudly. A few more minutes elapsed.

'Army!' one screamed. I heard a click. Two heads ducked together, Mother's and mine.

'Please, please do not shoot,' Mother pleaded loudly.

They calmed down significantly when they heard Mother's voice, realising in an instant that she had a Palestinian accent like them.

I was struck dumb with fear, but not Mother; she chatted kindly and gently with them, asked them where they were from, connected with them about Palestine, and filled in with her own Palestinian heritage. They warmed to her, and I relaxed somewhat and concentrated more on driving, especially when the heavy gun was lifted off my shoulder. When I found my voice, I asked them repeatedly where they wanted to be dropped off – I received no reply.

We came off the mountain road by joining the coastal one and headed south towards Sidon, in the opposite direction to Beirut and home. At the end of the longest two miles I had ever driven, all three shouted, 'STOP!'

I hit the brakes so fast, the car stopped dead.

They jumped out with their guns clanking behind them. In a flash, they darted like shadows across the road and disappeared into the dark night. The army was nowhere to be seen.

Immediately, I turned the car round in the middle of the road, put my foot on the accelerator and headed home without a backward look. I was a trembling wreck – my legs had turned to jelly, and I shivered and shook like a leaf. How I managed to drive the ten miles home, I don't know.

Thank God, the other car made it home safely.

Was it really true that the gunmen wanted to escape from the army chasing them? I knew full well that the army did not have a presence in that area. Or perhaps, was it a genuine kidnap attempt? Why did they try to get the passports from the women? Why did they get rid of the only male passenger in the car? Deep down in my heart I believed it was a genuine kidnap attempt, but something had driven me to confront the gunmen. The most atrocious, horrific killings, kidnappings and hostage-taking happened like this during the civil war. Where did my courage come from?

Thank you, Lord – for Mother being with us that day and calming them down, and for giving me the courage I needed to stand up to the gunmen.

What kept us going in these dangerous times was an undeniable sense of God's amazing presence and peace, protecting and taking care of us.

Who am I?

I was now in my thirties, had lived in Lebanon since I was five, and Lebanon was all I knew. I grew up identifying as a Lebanese. But the assurance of belonging, of being Lebanese, was shattered with the onslaught of the civil war. Up to 1975, I had been one of them, although deep down in my heart there was some disquiet. Gradually, I battled with the confused and painful question: the duality of my identity. Who was I? Where did I belong? Was this my country? Did the Lebanese want me any more? I was a single Christian Lebanese / Palestinian woman living in the Muslim part of Beirut. I was part of the Muslim side of the divided city of Beirut because I lived there, but it was the wrong enclave because I was a Christian. Which side did I belong to?

Abandoned!

Eastwood College was situated in Kfershima, a militia enclave on the outskirts of Beirut. Its headmistress was Hazel St John, and Wendy, a very gifted teacher, taught there. Wendy and I became good friends, and her friendship gave me the strength to keep going during the darkest, most frightening periods in the city. Travel between Kfershima and our home in West Beirut became very dangerous, so Wendy would often stay at our house for several days. Her encouragement and friendship, and especially her strong Christian faith and positive outlook on life, helped my faith grow; I learnt by watching her example. It was quite refreshing and inspiring in my confused culture.

We were all now at the mercy of the armed militias that ruled our lives and our streets. They formed themselves into mini armed units, governing the streets and controlling the local districts. There was no way out, and life became desperate, especially as all foreign embassies came to the conclusion that the civil war was getting worse and there was no end in sight. Evacuation of all foreign nationals was the priority of these embassies. They cared for their nationals, but no one in the world cared whether we lived or died. All the big powers took their hands off the mess that was Lebanon. We lived our days with a steel grip of anxiety, fear, hopelessness, dread and abandonment that choked the life out of us.

It wasn't enough that Lebanon disintegrated inwardly and became a failed state; externally, the country had to contend with fighting Israel, an additional and a very distressing and dangerous development. Fighting on all fronts embedded its tentacles into the core fabric of our society. The majority of Lebanese, at the end of the first year of the civil war, realised that the future of the country was doomed, prompting the immigration 'caravans' to roll out to Cyprus, to the rest of Europe, the USA and the UK. The result was that the country lost its best citizens when embassies, businesses, families and anyone who could leave joined the exodus.

As for me, the bottom fell out of my life when the British Embassy directed all its citizens to leave, while the Lebanese continued destroying their only inheritance, their country. The British realised that the end was nigh for Beirut and Lebanon as we knew it – doomed with all that it stood for: the centre of commerce, the meeting place between East and West. Its heritage was destroyed for ever. All multinational firms, from all over the globe, fled the area. Money and investments flew out of the country. My Palestinian extended family numbers dwindled to just a few families. All the others fled their second home.

As long as my foreign friends are still in Beirut, there is hope, I reassured myself. But as soon as the situation passed the no-return point, that glimmer of hope faded. Our foreign friends stayed with us as long as they could, not wanting to abandon us, but the time had come to leave the sinking ship. The city had become a very dangerous place for them to live in, and all abandoned Lebanon to its dark fate.

Beirut was very tense now as armed factions roamed the streets deciding who would live and who would die. For the last week, Wendy had stayed with us, as Kfershima, where she lived, was completely cut off. That morning she was due to fly out of Beirut, so I drove her to the International Hotel to get on the coach that would take her to the airport. We arrived at 9 am, and the coach was waiting outside the hotel. I was overcome by a wave of sadness, choked as I waved my goodbye when she got on with the others. Slowly, the coach pulled out, moved down the road and disappeared round the corner. They were gone. The searing pain, fear and agony of being abandoned was indescribable. They were free to get out of the inferno safely, while I was condemned to stay in my burning adopted home. Left behind, I got in the car and drove off, not seeing the road ahead of me as tears rolled down my cheeks. I got home to nurse my new fear, anxiety and despair.

I am on my own now, I told myself. *My friends have gone.*

The bottom of my life, as I knew it, fell out. What was I going to do? I could not imagine life without my LIVF friends' support; when life was so frightening, we had called each other, prayed and encouraged each other daily. My last hope – all that had kept me sane until then – was crushed when that coach disappeared down the street that morning. The outside world abandoned and forgot us, not caring whether we lived or died.

I had no one around me to call on who could help me in my deepest fear and distress. But then I remembered Mother's and my God, and cried out to Him in tears:

'God, I feel desolate. Will I ever get out of this horrifying nightmare? How can I live the rest of my life like this in danger, fear and despair? Lord, I'm so frightened, stressed and traumatised, and I can't see any hope. Please get me out of this desolate, hopeless, bleak and burning city.'

Still darkness closed in.

I was alone, left with only Mother around. The many friends I had, who were around before the start of the civil war, had left. The protective extended family units I had been surrounded by had emigrated. I was trapped and suffocated by fear, anxiety and by a culture I did not understand or want to be part of any more. I longed for a ray of hope, and when it came, I grasped it wholeheartedly. A friend who had emigrated to the UK a few months earlier invited me to apply for a job opportunity with his firm there, but the job interview was in Kuwait. Excitedly, I travelled to Kuwait for the three-day interview. Although I knew that if I accepted the offer I would get out of Beirut's hell, in the event I declined it as it was not the right job for me.

The Lord opened a second opportunity for me during another cease fire. I grasped the chance and got out of a paralysed, bombed-out city, and travelled to visit my sister and her family in peaceful Wakefield, England.

My first visit to the UK... What a wonderful country! I was so impressed by the calm, organised atmosphere, where law and order reigned and all were subject to the same rules. Human life was precious here, and what I had left behind was killing, death, anarchy, chaos, destruction, confusion, anxiety and hopelessness. During my two-week visit, over breakfast one morning, I read the small print of the job-advertising column in *The Times* newspaper. Lloyd's Register of Shipping was advertising for an Arabic speaker / translator to join their Middle East department in the City of London. What an opportunity! Encouraged by my sister and brother-in-law, I applied, went for the interview and was offered the job.

Really? I thought. *Am I going to get out of this horrifying nightmare? Am I going to be free of danger, stress, anxiety and the hopelessness of the future? Is it true? Yes, yes, yes!*

I was ecstatic. Not only did I have a new job but, more importantly, where was it based? London. My heart danced with the ray of hope. The offer of a prestigious job left me amazed. From burning Beirut to peaceful London. Out of all places, I was going to work in London!

Darkness lifted

Back in Beirut after my visit, I was overwhelmed by joy. I lived every day with a renewed hope, but it was only hope, and hope was not reality. The ferocious fighting still raged around us. I could not think of anything else except how to survive a day at a time. Mentally, emotionally and physically, daily life was a challenging struggle. We were still confined to our apartments. Normal life was completely paralysed.

Besides all these struggles, I had another. Slowly, slowly, the implications of what I was embarking on – a new life in London – dawned on me, and I was riddled with guilt. Mother was now in her seventies; was I going to leave her to fend for herself in a burning city?

Hasn't she suffered enough hardships and heartaches in bringing me and my sisters up? Didn't she selflessly sacrifice everything she had and knew to give us a better chance in life? Didn't she teach me to be resilient, strong and depend on no one else but myself? How can I abandon her now at this crucial time in her life, when she needs me most?

With my three sisters married and out of the country, I was the only one left in Beirut to look after her. I was indebted to her with my life.

There was no end to sleepless nights, anguish and confusion.

What do I do? Whom do I talk to? Who can show me the way?

My sisters, most of my extended family and my friends had already gone; but there was one still with me, looking after me: the God I trusted.

The miracle

For four months, I turned these issues over in my mind, seeking for a sign from God. I had been promised a work permit from Lloyd's Register of Shipping in London and waited desperately for it to arrive in Beirut. It never did. Hope faded completely when the whole country was cut off from the outside world. The airport and port closed, and all communications and services were cut during our darkest days of the civil war. My future depended on the work permit being sent to Beirut so I could present it to the authorities at Heathrow airport when I landed in the UK. It was my lifeline, and it was imperative that I had it in my hand.

One morning, I was brave enough to confront the perilous drive to the office at Gefinor Centre in Beirut. Nothing stirred in the streets, which were completely deserted after a bad night of shelling. I spent a few hours at work and then came back home. Mother greeted me with a big envelope in her hand. I looked at it briefly; it was covered with yellow and red stickers. I looked again – yes, it had my name on it. My heart missed a beat when I saw the sender's name. To my utter amazement and delight, it was the long-awaited work permit, together with a welcome letter from Lloyd's Register of Shipping in London. I hugged Mother and my joy was boundless.

Yes, it was the red and yellow covered, unmistakable worldwide postal delivery firm's envelope, DHL. Great! But hold on – wasn't the airport closed, the port out of action and all postal communication with the outside world non-existent? So how did this envelope arrive at my address in a bombed-out city? To this day, the mystery of how that work permit arrived is beyond any logical explanation.

I can only say one thing: I trusted God and he was working, looking after my future.

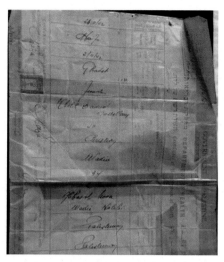

Palestinian birth certificate, 1942 D.O.B.

The refugee family's journey.

Ground floor home on Abbas St., Haifa. Building owned by my uncle.

Temple of Bacchus / Jupiter, Baalbeck.

Lebanon ration card. Address: Wavell Refugee Camp.

Hajar el Hibla (pregnant woman stone, Baalbeck).

*The family in 1950.
Left to right: Iptissam, Siham,
Huda, Mother and me.*

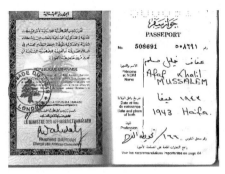

Lebanese passport, 1943 D.O.B.

*Our garden where Blackie was
found.*

Bombed downtown Beirut.

*Playing with Blackie on house
roof.*

*Bullets shells collected from street
in front of our building.*

Newspaper cutting of fire.

Times Portfolio card.

St George's Monastery, Wadi Kelt.

St George's Cathedral, Jerusalem.

Emile Habiby, writer and Knesset member, 1922-1996.

Sitting in Scud missile shelter (bathroom).

'Scottie' by Sarah Dye.

Elijah Trust / Gill Dye visiting cards.

"Don't wait any longer!"

'JAFFA, Jesus, a friend for all' sign.

Jaffa directors – opening day.

Jaffa Orchard coffee shop – before and after.

Jaffa Orchard coffee shop postcard.

5

Finding Peace

LONDON, UK – 1976

I worked at Lloyd's Register of Shipping for a year and a half, and I admit it wasn't plain sailing. Although I spoke the language, in many ways London felt very foreign to me. More than anything else, I was struck by the engulfing silence as I walked down the street or rode on the tube. The lack of sunshine, and cold days around three quarters of the year, left me physically, mentally and emotionally cold. I asked myself, *Don't people know each other like they do in Beirut? Have they lost the most important function to humans: speaking and talking to each other?* Nobody knew anybody and nobody wanted to know anybody in public places. It was such a contrast. When I walked down the streets in Beirut, there was a vibrancy, an enthusiasm for life, with the sun shining, warming people's minds and hearts. Everyone had something to say.

On the other hand, I had joined a fabulous country. I was enthralled by the inbuilt discipline and respect for law and order, which is part of my upbringing and personality, but unfortunately very foreign to my culture – and was non-existent during the civil war. I noticed small, endearing touches. For example, when driving, I stopped at a junction and let the other car get through first; I got a raised hand in appreciation instead of a raised one with a gun!

I guess the high price paid for being so considerate to others is to lose one's natural bent to live a selfish life. I learnt to say thank you, please and excuse me with every breath I took. In Beirut my breathing was well spaced between each one of these, as I used them sparingly and selectively. A difference of cultural norms.

One of the joys of living and working in London was going to the theatre and concerts. The most memorable one was the concert I attended with some of my Beirut friends at the Albert Hall soon after I arrived. At the end of a fantastic musical evening and with the last note played, I woke up suddenly, froze and trembled to exploding cannons. Clapping hands brought me back from my daydreaming reverie to the reality of Tchaikovsky's *1812*. Thank the Lord I was in London and not in Beirut!

I commuted to work from Highbury (where I shared a flat with Clare, a friend I had met at All Souls Church) to my destination, Fenchurch Street in the City. It included a drive to the tube station, a hop on the Piccadilly Line at Arsenal, then changing to the Northern Line, arriving at Bank Station. Commuting was an activity so unfamiliar and foreign to me, in contrast to using my car to travel even for very short walking distances in Beirut. I learnt and copied what people did here. When I mentioned my need for a book to Clare, she said, 'I have the right thing for you,' and duly produced *Watership Down*.

I had not read a book for a long time, and as there was no other book, I welcomed its company. Soon the rabbits became my close friends on these journeys and filled the emptiness created by lack of human conversations. I was impressed one day when I received a letter at work with this address: *Miss Afaf Musallam, Lloyds Register of Shipping, London.* It had been sent by a friend in Beirut. I call that efficiency! I also enjoyed the week's highlight: lunchtime meetings at St Helen's, Bishopsgate. One week our speaker was Chuck Colson, President Nixon's aide who had been imprisoned for being implicated in Watergate. I was specially impacted by his message on forgiveness and reconciliation.

After a year working at Lloyds Register of Shipping, I gladly accepted my Beirut boss's invitation to join their newly opened offices on Park Lane. During the interview, I remember him telling me that he had also opened an office in Paris. He commented on the two nations by saying that neither the French nor the English particularly like and welcome foreigners. But the difference between the two is that the French will tell you to your face, while the Brits will keep it to themselves!

'Get to know folk for forty days; you either become one of them or wander away from them' – an Arabic proverb depicting my general situation! So I moved from Lloyd's in the City to working as the director's assistant at a new Middle Eastern company in Mayfair. Both businesses needed an Arabic speaker to facilitate their work, so the precious work permit status was easily transferred from one firm to the other. I felt much more at ease working with a people and a culture I was familiar with.

I enjoyed my new job and London life. I had found a good church and had a group of close friends. When I had time off, I visited my sister and her family in Wakefield, which was a great blessing and encouragement to me.

When I first arrived, it had been a great relief to leave war-torn Beirut for the peace and stability of the UK. But after a year and a half, I found myself feeling unsettled. I felt increasingly responsible for Mother being on her own, except for a cousin and an uncle as the only family support nearby. In addition, I picked up the phone one day and my sister told me that she and her husband Ron were on the move; in four weeks' time they were leaving the UK for Sri Lanka, where Ron had been offered a job. These two things, together with the well-paid but uninteresting job, left me unsatisfied with my life and contributed to a feeling that something was still missing.

Then one Sunday, surprisingly, I had an unexpected conversation with John Stott, a well-known, respected and influential author in Christian circles and rector of All Souls Church. He was at the door saying goodbye to people leaving the service. As he shook my hand he said:

'I have a special message for you from Colin Chapman. I saw him last week in Beirut.' Then he gave me Colin's letter.

Colin was the Regional Secretary of IFES – the International Fellowship of Evangelical Students – and I was amazed at his invitation asking me rejoin the LIVF team in Beirut as the national staff worker. This was no coincidence but a crystal clear direction from the One who cared for me. I had trusted Him to show me my next step, and He did.

Beirut, here I come... but with one deep regret: the date I travelled back to Beirut I had been invited to attend tennis at Wimbledon. I love tennis, and I was disappointed that I was unable to go. (However, in 2012, thirty-four years later, I received an invitation from a friend to go to the Olympics tennis as my seventieth birthday gift. What a great experience – and a great lesson to learn: that God does not withhold any good thing from us, but He gives them in his own timing and not ours.)

So I packed my bags and landed at Beirut International Airport on 30th July 1978. I was so much looking forward to the challenging new job, forgetting all the difficult issues that came with it. Lawlessness was still rife, and politically the country was still very unstable, but the country was now calmer. The bigger issue I still grappled with was trying to establish who I was and where I belonged. Was this another stage in the process of finding out?

6

Back to Beirut

BEIRUT, LEBANON – 1978

Working with LIVF as the Lebanese staff worker was a great blessing to me, as I really enjoyed working with university students. We had seen the continued growth of the student movement since it had first been established ten years previously. We had just opened the Student Centre near the American University, and not very far from Beirut University College. A flat spacious enough to accommodate all LIVF activities, it was the perfect venue. Once a month, students from universities and church groups attended lectures on subjects relating to their daily living and faith. In addition, discussion Bible study groups were held during the week. On the social scene, lunches on Thursdays were a great informal get-together for all students, staff and volunteers. The Centre, at any given time, was full of vibrant student chatter and laughter; a much-needed zest which aided our everyday struggles, lifting our lives above uncertainty, unrest and civil war.

The Centre was on the second floor of a three-storey building with a small front garden, situated in the fashionable Hamra district of West Beirut. A short garden path led to a lobby and staircase. The Centre front door was always kept open, a sign of welcome to all students coming in. On entering the spacious flat, a big hall was on the left; next, there was a large kitchen; and my office was tucked in on the right.

At the end of one month, strapped for cash, I collected my cheque and nipped to the bank / post office round the corner when I had a minute. I cashed the cheque and put all the money in my purse in my bag. (Middle East culture at this stage used cash in most dealings.) I returned quickly and carried on preparing for the afternoon Bible study. That went very well. It was 6 pm, time to go home; with the other volunteers and staff, I tidied up the Centre, got my bag from the desk drawer and took my car keys out. Something was missing! Where was my purse? I looked everywhere, again and again, inside, under, behind the drawer, on the desk, under the desk, but found nothing. Maybe I had misplaced it; I asked around but no one had seen it. I got more and more agitated, as I had lost my month's income. What was I going to do? The sad realisation dawned on me that there had either been a pickpocket at the post office or someone had taken it from my bag in the drawer. The dire economic situation in the country during these days had made such occurrences very common incidents.

The next morning, I found the purse thrown in the garden, empty. One mystery was solved: the theft had taken place at the Centre, not at the post office. I had been naive and very trusting, not locking my drawer.

On my way home two days later, I was handed an envelope by a colleague saying, 'This was donated by students and colleagues; we hope this will help.'

When I counted the money, I was flabbergasted, as the amount in the envelope was the exact amount of my month's salary. The amazing thing is that no one knew what my salary was and what other people had contributed.

I was so relieved, thankful and reassured that even in those very unstable and anxious times, I was not on my own but had very generous and caring friends.

The last chance

As we were still living with all the political instability and security issues surrounding us, we all learnt how to exist as normally as possible whatever the situation was. We adjusted to a wide range of restrictions and limitations on movement, avoiding dangerous roads and areas. However, we concentrated on what we could do or accomplish on any given day or task. At this time, LIVF was embarking on its biggest programme yet: preparing for the Middle East student conference at Ayia Napa in Cyprus.

I woke up on that particular day with a sense of excitement and anticipation. At the Centre, I booked airline tickets and checked all arrangements were in order for the twenty-five students who were joining us from all over the Middle East.

At midday I received an urgent call from my uncle Naim, asking me to meet him that afternoon for coffee, to discuss an important matter of personal interest. When he realised I was too busy, he was happy to tell me over the phone:

'Afaf, I have this banker friend, Christian background, who is well off and owns a villa in Greece. He is a very nice, gentle person and he does not smoke. His bank has relocated him to Athens due to the unrest in Beirut and he is looking for a wife – a wife like yourself, decent, educated and quiet, with a good family background. I know that he will provide adequately for you. The other thing you need to know is that he was married but there are no children and he has recently got divorced.'

I went quiet for a minute and a thought flicked through my mind: *Isn't this my chance to marry well, settle down and escape uncertainty, fear, danger, anxiety and the burning city?* Instantly, though, alarm bells started ringing. *Did he say divorced? Yes, he did!* Was I prepared to marry a divorced man? This was something unacceptable both in my culture and according to my understanding at that time of what the Bible teaches – but Uncle would not take no for an answer.

My youngest uncle was always the one to 'arrange' anything and everything where the family was concerned. To convince me and to present a stronger argument, he also did not forget to emphasise and remind me that I was in my thirties, still not married, and might not have a better offer or chance of marriage than this. My answer was:

'Uncle, if he is not a committed Christian, I am not interested.'

The Middle East student conference at Ayia Napa was a success, reinforcing my decision in turning down my uncle's generous marriage offer! No regrets lingered after that.

All Beirut lost count of how many ceasefires came into effect to be broken immediately. These were usually followed by intense fighting spreading from Beirut to all other parts of Lebanon. The whole small country was split into neighbouring villages and towns fighting each other. The weapons arsenal included, for the first time, tanks and anti-tank missiles used in narrow street fighting. Coupled with this escalation, the intensity of the Israeli daily air strikes systematically flattened and demolished whole tall buildings, homes of up to twenty-four families, on top of the residents' heads, erasing our belief in humanity.

Where do we go?

During 1979, I was blessed by being invited as the Lebanese staff worker to the IFES General Assembly conference held every four years, this time in Norway. Because of the divided city and the continued fighting in Beirut, I was not able to collect my visa from the embassy on the other side of the Green Line. The intense sniper fire between the Christian and Muslim sectors made it impossible. The flight to Oslo was in the afternoon. The day had arrived and I still did not have my visa. I would not have made it but for one brave, mad taxi driver, courageous or desperate, who drove me at breakneck speed through deserted streets lined with ruined, towering office buildings. I spent twenty minutes in sheer terror, sitting in the back slumped in my seat, listening to sniper gun fire round us. We arrived shattered but without being hit. I collected my visa from the embassy, and from there we followed safe roads straight to the airport. I got on the plane just in time for take-off.

What a memorable conference that was! For the first time in my life, and with Colin's encouragement, I shared with about four hundred people that I was a Christian, a Palestinian refugee. By speaking publicly, I acknowledged and accepted myself for who I really was. I must admit, it was a very uncomfortable and emotional experience. But nevertheless, it was the first step on my long journey to the restoration of my identity. I am glad I was able to share my testimony and people did not reject me because I was a Palestinian, but accepted me as a Christian Palestinian.

I had been working with LIVF for the last three years, and there was still no sign that the end of the civil war was in sight. I was becoming increasingly unsettled, emotionally and mentally, as life had not returned to normal in the way I had hoped, and I was missing my friends who had left. So I started exploring other job avenues. I was amazed at the unexpected event that happened next.

Cousin Mazen, the owner of the building we lived in, asked me to see him 'on an important matter'. He began:

'Afaf, you know that I am the last person who would leave this country, but danger, the unstable political situation and the fierce fighting have finally driven me to emigrate. I am really frightened of staying, and I must think of my family's safety and future. We are emigrating to the States, and I have already sold the building with the twenty-four flats. That means you and your mother will have to vacate the flat by the end of the month and look for somewhere else to live.'

He knew that there was no prospect or hope of our moving anywhere else. His father, Mother's brother, had rented the flat to us for a token rent, and any other flat in a reasonably safe part of Beirut was beyond our means.

'But please, don't worry,' he continued. 'I had thought of this and would like to offer you LP80,000 (£10,000 in the 1980s) to help you and your mother move and find another place.'

I had no savings of my own, nor did Mother have a penny to her name. Social security did not exist in Lebanon in those days. Being the only breadwinner, my existence had always been hand-to-mouth. I had never owned a fraction of that amount.

I looked at him with wide, unbelieving eyes and a big smile on my face, unable to contain my joy and astonishment.

'Mazen, thank you so much for your generous offer. You don't realise it, but what you have just said has confirmed my decision and helped my permanent relocation plans.' I beamed at him.

It was his turn to look at me with wide eyes. A big smile on his face, he enquired:

'Where are you going? When are you leaving and does your mother know about your plans?'

'No, but now, given your plans to emigrate and your generous financial offer, you have made it so much easier for me to tell her of my own plan to leave for good. Thank you so much; at least now she will be more willing to consider leaving Beirut, knowing that you will not be around,' I replied confidently.

Up to that moment, no one knew, not even Mother, that I had applied for my previous job back in Park Lane, London, and that I had been offered it and had accepted the offer. I had known that as long as Mazen and his family were still in Beirut, Mother would be unwilling to even think of leaving.

Was the perfect timing of all these events a coincidence? Were they events that happened randomly? I don't believe so. They were God's plan.

The challenge of tackling yet another move, together with a demanding new job in another country, filled me with excitement, joy and anticipation, though mixed with a measure of fear. I loved following and trusting the Lord's challenges, leading me into the next chapter of my life.

During my last weeks in Lebanon and after working four years with LIVF, from 1978 to 1982, I reflected on the big part Lebanon InterVarsity Fellowship had played in my life. Not only that, it had been a landmark, a turning point on the road towards finding my identity. It had also been a landmark in the history of LIVF, since the three LIVF founding members – Antoine Haddad, Mary Mikhail and I – felt it was the right time to submit an application from LIVF to register the association as a charity with the Lebanese government, no matter what the security issues were in the country.

Lebanon's civil war stretched beyond its eleventh year, and by this time the armed Palestinian presence had become a force to be reckoned with in the country. Besides the unimaginable destruction from inside and from outside the country, the continued Syrian systematic invasion and occupation completed the cycle of Lebanon's demise.

7

Miraculous Provisions

It was sad to say my goodbyes to all my dear LIVF friends, colleagues and students in Beirut during my farewell party. Likewise, there were heartbreaking goodbyes to extended family members, knowing that some I might not see again. I knew this was it, this was for good, I wasn't coming back to Lebanon. This chapter of my life was on its last page. Leaving Mother behind was the hardest thing to bear, although I trusted God for her safety and I was reassured that Cousin Mazen and family were still in Beirut at that time.

Nevertheless, I clung to this Bible verse, a promise to give me a home and a future, given to me by Colin Chapman before I left: *'They found no city to dwell in ... then they cried out to the LORD ... and He delivered them out of their distress... He led them forth by the right way that they might go to a city for a dwelling place.'* (Psalm 107:4-7, NKJV)

I was forty years old, a single woman embarking on a life-changing venture. So on Saturday, 16th January 1982, I packed my bags for the last time in our flat in Beirut. I was in a daze as I waited for my cousin's car to arrive to take me to the airport. I felt it must be someone else who was hugging Mother goodbye, tears streaming down my face and a lump in my throat. I kissed her, but inside I was torn and devastated – how was I going to leave her to fend on her own in a bombed-out city? A wave of sorrow flooded my inner being; I knew that the security I had had in my family and friends in Beirut – the second home I had known – had gone forever.

The car was waiting. For the last time, I looked up towards the third floor balcony, my home for twenty years, and said my silent goodbye. On the pavement stood a slim, frail figure. I kissed Mother again and got in the car, choking on my tears. When was I going to see her again? I did not know. I could not take my eyes off the lonely, slim figure standing on the pavement as the car moved slowly then gathered pace. The last thing I saw was her small hand waving me on. I waved back, hot tears coming down faster, blurring her from my sight. Then we lost each other.

At Beirut airport, I got on the plane with a very heavy heart. 'Am I really, really leaving for good?' There was still time to get off the plane and go back to what I knew best and be with Mother. For a long time afterwards, the lonely figure standing on the pavement waving me goodbye did not leave me, because I was so confused and torn, wondering whether I should have stayed to look after her rather than leaving her behind to face a fate of loneliness and danger on her own. I was turning my back on all that was familiar and was a part of me. But was that God's opening and hope, for me to pursue a new future and life? I believe it was. It was an unknown and exciting future, if not a frightening one.

For the four-hour flight, I was in a daze reflecting on all these matters. I came to when the captain's voice came over the intercom:

'Ladies and Gentlemen, we are now approaching Heathrow airport, and we will be landing in ten minutes.'

I looked out of the small window as the plane broke through thick dark clouds and slowly descended; it hovered over a landscape of a beautiful patchwork of different shades of green and brown. The airport came into view, the 'no smoking' sign lit up, the engine noise grew louder and louder, and the tarmac came towards the plane and joined the captain in his welcome as we met the earth with a sudden jolt. The huge plane taxied slowly, shuddered and then went silent.

'Welcome to London,' the captain's voice came over again.

My heart missed a beat, with excitement lifting the heaviness I had felt during the flight.

I had been forced out from my home country and had become a refugee. I had been forced out of my first adoptive country by bullets and a civil war. Not this one. What a contrast! What a welcome from my second, peaceful adoptive country. Joy welled up inside me as I sent up a silent prayer of thanks to God, who had opened the way for me to come here. My joy was complete when my sister and her family met me in the arrival hall at 20.15 on 16th January 1982.

After a week of settling in at Claire's, my friend from All Souls Church, in Hanwell, I started work as a personal assistant to one of the company's directors in Mayfair. This time round it was much more straightforward, as my previous two years working in London, from 1976 to 1978, had given me a good grounding in the British way of life.

Initially, I wanted to live in London, near where I was working, and found a house to buy near Claire's apartment in Hanwell. However, I pulled out of the deal, losing my deposit, after I considered that my sister Siham and I were ultimately responsible for Mother's welfare in her old age. It seemed right to invite Mother to come and join us in the UK. So, we knew we needed a larger house to accommodate Siham's young family, who had already settled in Bedford, and Mother, who would live with them when she joined us from Beirut. Although I had wanted to be completely independent of the family, reluctantly I agreed that a shared home was best for all of us.

The search for a big house started. Like me, my brother-in-law Ron worked in London, and we would commute daily by train. We had a chance to look at *32, The Embankment*, which was up for sale. We all agreed that it was a big house and ideal for all our needs. Its beautiful position and its big garden by the River Ouse left us with no doubt that it was the right house for us all.

We showed our interest and were in the negotiating stage with the owners. However, we were shocked when, one Sunday, one of the free papers had a picture of the house on fire on its first page. The fire was restricted to the unused top floor which was to be my flat. Nevertheless, we put in an offer, which was accepted. 30th August 1983 arrived, and we moved into the big house with a lot of excitement and celebrations. At one point, we all stood in the garden, opened a champagne bottle and the cork flew and entered straight through my third floor open window! Afterwards we prayed and thanked God, dedicating the house and our time together to Him. My friend Wendy was a great help in the process of decorating my flat as I wanted it. It was great fun. An added blessing at this time was that I did not have to pay a penny towards all the decorating and renovating expenses, since the seller's insurance money covered it all. *What a gift! Thank you, Lord, for You met my need.*

To crown it all, now that I had got my beautiful home in Bedford, my boss was relocating and gave me some of his lovely, expensive furniture as a gift. Every time I look at those items in my home, I am thankful and reminded of his generosity.

By now I had applied for a visa for Mother, but it had not been granted so she was still in Beirut. We were very concerned for her safety and welfare. She had absolutely no income of her own, and I would transfer an amount to her every month to live on. But after an incident when she blacked out and went out into the street disorientated, asking people if they had seen her daughter Afaf, we knew we had a crisis on our hands. Not only that but worse was to come: on 6th June 1982, Israel invaded Lebanon with a massive land and air assault and laid siege to West Beirut. The bombardment to destroy the Palestinian Liberation Organisation, the PLO, was relentless and many died.

The thought of Mother being stuck on her own in her flat for days on end during the invasion filled me with anguish. We prayed about the situation, and Siham and Ron applied to the Home Office for Mother to come to the UK and live with them. They were devastated when it was refused. Not to be put off, they appealed against the Home Office's ruling and filed a new application, with an accompanying letter from their MP.

Meanwhile in Beirut, my cousin Mazen made sure that Mother was safe and out of the country before he finally left for good. He got her on a plane with a French visa and sent her to stay with my sister Iptissam, her husband Scott and their family in St Ismier, near Grenoble. That was not a long-term solution, and with still no word from the Home Office regarding the appeal, we all dedicated one particular day to pray. Not long after that, the answer came in a dramatic way. While my sister's church house group were actually in a prayer meeting for Mother's situation, Ron came in with the Home Office's response in his hand – it was a yes. Mother was granted a residential visa on humanitarian grounds. A cheer of thanks went up to the Lord. Her joining us in the UK in June 1983 was miraculous, the answer to all our prayers. Mother and all of us were so amazed, and marvelled at all these events, how they had unfolded and with such precision timing. There was great rejoicing when Mother joined us in the big house. We thanked God for his love and mercy in getting her safe out of Beirut at the crucial time and for the Home Office allowing her to come and live with us.

For a few years I had been working in London, commuting the fifty miles to and from Bedford each day. My days were marked by extreme tiredness, boredom, emptiness, a lacklustre existence and missed opportunities to enjoy other activities in Bedford because I was so exhausted. When I first arrived, life had been full of promise and hope. What a contrast! Now I existed like a zombie: waking up, leaving the house at 6:30 and returning in the evening at 7:30 as exhausted as when I had left. There was no escaping the drudgery of the killing routine. I could only find another job nearer home and escape commuting when my five years were up and I was granted an indefinite stay. My work permit allowed me to work as a personal assistant with only that particular company in Park Lane. Another two long years...

Financially, I was living at the very edge; commuting was very expensive plus very high mortgage payments left, very little of my salary to satisfy the demands of living on my own.

Under the chair

Please come with me to the Chinese Restaurant in Leicester Square in London. I went with six of my office colleagues for a meal there. First, I was worried if I could afford it, and second, I was not sure I would like the food as it would be my first time having a Chinese meal. But I overcame my hesitation and went in some trepidation. We were shown our reserved table of eight, a long thin table. I pulled out my chair to sit down, and exactly under it there was a bundle. I picked it up, and yes, you have guessed it, there was £25 in wrapped notes. I was able to pay for my delicious lunch, and my anxiety of being out of pocket the rest of the month was unfounded. I have no doubt in my mind whatsoever that this was another gift from a generous Father.

'No good thing does He withhold from those who walk uprightly.' (Psalm 84:11)

Outside the grocer's shop

I was so tired now of commuting to London every day to work to make ends meet that I resorted to staying at the YMCA in London, sharing a flat there. I would stay in London on weekdays and drive home to Bedford for the weekend. It did help for a short while. At the end of one of these weekends, I drove to London, arrived around 7 pm on the Sunday, and went to visit my minister's wife who was in a London hospital. At 9 pm, and before retiring to the shared flat at the YWCA, I went into a grocer's shop opposite and bought the next day's breakfast. I walked out of the shop and was just outside the door when I nearly stepped on it: a tied bundle (another one!) on the ground. I knelt and picked it up. Yes, it was a bundle of bank notes. This time I wasn't at a loss, because at that precise moment two policemen walked towards me. Without thinking, I blurted out:

'I picked up this outside the grocer's and don't know what to do with it.'

Both looked at me strangely – anyway, they took the bundle from me and counted the money. It came to £60, and they gave me a receipt.

'In two months' time, if no one has claimed it, we will send you a cheque for the amount,' they said.

I went satisfied by the result, thinking that would be the end of the story. Amazingly, three weeks later, I received a cheque in the post for the £60. Thank you, Lord! I was pleased and treated the family for a meal on the Bedford riverboat in a well-deserved celebration of God's goodness.

Gifts from above

It was another early morning when my sister took Ron and me to Bedford Station. We caught the seven o'clock train, and in another three quarters of an hour we arrived at St Pancras Station. Ron and I parted company as I took the underground to Green Park Station. Finally, using my God-given transport mode, my journey ended in a nine-minute walk to *49 Mount Street, Mayfair*. It was 9 a.m.

Another day at the office!

The offices occupied three floors. The basement housed the administrative offices. The ground floor had all four directors with their personal assistants' offices. The first floor had no tenants and was not occupied at the time. All four directors' offices were connected by a long corridor, with all its windows overlooking and opening onto a large sky-well in the middle of the building. The basement offices were visible from the ground and first-floor office windows above.

On that particular day, I was on duty to open up before the others arrived. I unlocked the main door, entered, switched off the alarm, switched on the lights and walked along the corridor, passing two directors' offices on my left. I turned right to my office which led to my boss's office. My desk was next to the window that opened also onto, and overlooked, the sky-well. I put the key in to unlock the window to let fresh air in, when something caught my eye on the windowsill outside the locked window. Astonished, I heard my voice:

'What is that!?'

I looked again. It seemed to me like a wad of paper – but was it? I wasn't sure! I opened the window, stretched out my hand and retrieved the bundle. I was stunned, horrified, dumbfounded, frightened, amazed and shaken when I picked up the tightly wrapped bank notes and sat down while talking to myself.

'How did this money get there? How did it get on the outside of a locked windowsill? Who and why would anyone put money on a sill? Money falling accidentally from an upstairs window is illogical – no one is upstairs.'

Not knowing what to do, I put the £90 in my drawer, still trying to figure out a plausible explanation. I waited all day for the riddle's solution from somewhere, but none came.

I went home in the evening and, true to my introvert nature, did not share this bizarre incident with the family. I kept it to myself, thinking that was that – end of story.

The next morning, I arrived again early to open up. I followed the same routine. I entered my office and avoided looking at the window, but not for long. My heart missed a beat. Extraordinarily, the same shape was on the windowsill outside the locked window. Horrified, I mumbled:

'It cannot be... Twice?!'

Automatically, I unlocked and opened the window, retrieving the rolled-up notes. Baffled and anxious, I laid the £100 next to the previous day's find. During the business of the day, between phone calls and arranging meetings, the thought about what had happened was lurking at the back of my mind. I tried very hard not to think of it but could not completely forget. I waited all day, longing to hear something that would explain its existence. None came. Still, I was not brave enough to mention it to anyone at the office or at home. I would look ridiculous if I did, wouldn't I? So I kept it to myself.

I came to the office the third morning, wondering if I might find the same. Loudly, I said to myself:

'Please, Lord, no more. I can't handle it.'

To my relief there was nothing on the windowsill the third morning. A sigh of relief escaped my lips. My dilemma was, if I told people that I had found bank notes on the outside of my locked windowsill – not once, but twice – who would believe me? I would look foolish and be ridiculed. But then, why would anyone put them there when they could have given them to me directly if they wanted to? And as to their having fallen from the upstairs window, there was no chance; the upstairs was locked and had no occupants. For me, there was only one plausible explanation: it was very clear that this was a gift from above. My Father chose to give me his gift this way when I needed it most, so I accepted it with no questions asked but with thankfulness instead.

After a twenty-year period, I broke my silence and shared what had happened with my family. Now, I am sharing it with you. Why didn't I keep my silence for good? Because now I have the courage and maturity to share what God had done for me; I have accepted that it was a gift from God, and if He chose to supplement my salary like this, who am I to question the way He did it? I am just grateful and amazed at His generous, practical and loving care. As it turned out, this was far from the last of such gifts.

Thank you, 'Father Christmas'

I flew downstairs, my heart pounding fast, skipping two steps at a time – I was younger then! – from my top floor flat to my sister's family room on the ground floor. I could not hide my excitement as I asked my sister, brother-in-law and mother to check my sums.

It was Christmas 1984, a very special Christmas. Life was hectic but the weekends provided rest, joy and recovery. I cherished every minute of being in my lovely flat with its beautiful views.

This Saturday was a special day: it was a cold, crispy morning in December, but the sun shone and its rays penetrated through the French windows overlooking the River Ouse, warming my heart and my flat. I woke up that morning with the strangest of feelings, a glow of excitement and anticipation which filled me with joy and a deep contentment. It was a long time since I had felt like this, and I remember it still as if it were yesterday. You know the feeling, when deep down you know that something big is going to happen...

I sat at the glass table in the window alcove, admiring the beautiful scenery in front of me. The tall trees partly obscured the view from my third-floor windows in summer – but not today; they stood leafless, exposing the beauty of the effortlessly flowing river. The elegant white swans glided over the river to their daily feeding places. I gazed out of the window lost in thought. At that moment, I attributed the strange, calm feeling I felt to the wonderful scene out of my window. Yes, that was one reason for it, and another was that it was the best day of the week; I did not have to travel to London to a boring job. (There was no running away from my hand-to-mouth existence as my salary went straight onto mortgage repayments and train fares. With no bank balance behind me to fall onto, money was very tight, but I was thankful for all the blessings I had, especially having Mother and my sister's family downstairs.)

Another Saturday luxury was reading *The Times* newspaper, borrowed from the family. I read it at my leisure, then checked my card numbers against what was printed in the paper. This was a stocks and shares game called 'Portfolio' that *The Times* was running during the Christmas period. I was working and familiar with the names of all stocks and shares on the London Stock Market, so I thought that it would be fun to play. I checked the numbers on my card against the numbers printed in the newspaper. I checked them once, checked them twice, checked them three times... I kept adding them again and again. Every time I got the same sum as the newspaper's; they all matched! I could not believe my eyes.

Had I won? Could this be true? It dawned on me that I really had won the prize. I ran downstairs two steps at a time, my heart pounding, out of breath but beaming with excitement. I asked my sister, brother-in-law and Mother to check my sums. We all sat down and checked them repeatedly. Yes, they all matched. The family verified my adding skills and confirmed that my sums were correct. My joy had no bounds. But how much did I win? That day's prize was £20,000. Immediately I rang the newspaper and claimed the prize. They congratulated me and wished me a Happy Christmas. The local newspaper put it on their front page: 'Thank you, Santa'. I added, 'Thank you, *God*, for helping me out financially.' *What a wonderful Christmas gift! How can I doubt Him now? Thank you, my Father.*

As I am writing about all these events now, I am amazed; but I never questioned them then, just accepted them as extraordinary incidents helping me towards maturity in my everyday Christian life. I knew that God cared for me because He knew my needs and satisfied them.

My Christian faith was strengthened at Russell Park Baptist Church in Bedford. Three things cemented me to RP, as it was known. First, our minister closed his prayers with an endearing 'ameen' as said in Arabic, instead of the English 'amen'. Second, both he and his wife showed me genuine Christian care and affection. But really what cemented my belonging to this church were the welcoming friendships of many there, especially someone called Joy. She invited me to lunch the second Sunday I was there. I made many more friends, their friendships lasting to this present day. Together we enjoyed trips, outings and conferences, and I took part in the church's many regular activities. The support of these friends was priceless for many years to come.

Citizenship / birth certificate

For my first five years in the UK, I was on a work permit visa, which meant I could not change my job and every year I had to go to the Home Office in Croydon to renew it. The fifth year arrived, and I was granted an 'Indefinite Leave to Remain' permit. That meant I was free to change jobs if I wanted to and apply to become a British citizen. Towards this, my boss asked the firm's solicitor to complete all the formalities and submit my application to become a British subject.

There was a little complication in my application due to the discrepancy of my two conflicting birth dates. Where I was born in Haifa, Palestine, my birth certificate's date was 1942, but I had lived with 1943 registered on all my official papers in Lebanon and in the UK. How did such a mix-up occur? Well, when we became refugees in Lebanon in 1948, Mother simply forgot when I was born and made the mistake. She did not have our birth certificates with her to remind her as she had left them behind in the house when we fled. Ten years later, my grandmother brought them with her when she joined us in Beirut from Haifa. She rescued them from the street, where the Jewish family had thrown them when they took over our home. We were surprised by Mother's mistake, but no one attempted to rectify it, due to the complexity of these issues in the Lebanese courts. Anyway, what was the problem of being one year younger than my real age? I did not see any and it did not bother me, so I did nothing to put it right.

But now in 1988, when I applied for British citizenship, the Home Office wanted to know the reason for the discrepancy between the two dates. They were very understanding when I explained the situation, and issued my British citizenship with the correct date of 1942 instead of 1943. What were the implications? Mine was the only forty-seventh birthday on this earth to be missed! I grew up two years in one go, from being a forty-six-year-old to becoming a forty-eight-year-old. This was highly significant later on. I don't believe this was a coincidence but another step on the road map where the Master Planner showed me that He was in control of my life and I had nothing to fear.

I looked forward to visiting the solicitor's offices to complete the citizenship application, where I was to sign and take my oath of allegiance to the Queen. I imagined a ceremony, sitting down at a round table and taking the oath with my hand on the Bible. Far from it! The papers were on top of a filing cabinet, I signed them quickly and with no ceremony at all. I was greatly disappointed, but it did not change anything; I was now part of this great nation, a fully-fledged British citizen. I felt proud and thankful, having taken another step towards belonging and integration.

I was grateful to my firm when they covered all of the solicitors' costs and official fees.

Three years passed and I was still in the same job, commuting to London. Although I was very thankful to have work, I felt frustrated, wasting my time doing something that bored me. In other words, what I was doing was not filling the emptiness I felt. I wonder what I would have chosen if I had been given a choice between the hopelessness of the civil war in Lebanon or the loneliness I felt in England. I think the choice would have been a difficult one!

I knew I had to do something drastic, so with no regrets, I resigned from my job in 1989 with no other job to go to.

Trip of a lifetime

What a relief and what a release! The noose was off – it had been round my neck strangling me. I had held that job for seven years and now I was liberated. What a joy to be free, with no pressure, no long journeys, no trains to catch and no deadlines to meet. All my anxieties evaporated. It was a pleasure to get up at any time I wanted and potter around my lovely flat; I met up with friends and did all the things I had missed doing before. The few idle months were great but passed very quickly. I still had to pay monthly bills and mortgage payments. So for a few months, I did temporary administration work in Bedford and Cambridge. At the same time, I knew I needed time to find out what the Lord wanted me to spend the rest of my life doing.

Now that I was working as a temp and not tied up with a contract, together with having a new British passport, I was free to travel anywhere. Previously, as a Palestinian or Lebanese, my travel movements had been restricted; I had not been able to visit Haifa in Israel, my birthplace. Now the opportunity to do so presented itself, and on 17th August 1990, Wendy and I boarded a British Airways flight to Tel Aviv to start a remarkable two-week holiday. On arrival we hired a car and drove to Jerusalem, staying at St George's Guest House in East Jerusalem. This was part of the Palestinian Middle Eastern Christian Diocese and also a place where pilgrims from all over the world were welcomed. What a beautiful place, with the Anglican cathedral taking centre stage of the compound! During our stay we met many people, both Palestinians and British – among them, Peter Crooks, the dean of the cathedral. I learnt from him that the current British manager of the guest house – a twenty-four-bed guest house – was leaving, and they were looking for a new manager to replace her.

Was this the challenge I needed? I had the advantage of being both a British subject and a Palestinian Christian. The idea attracted me as it was people-oriented, and Peter evidently picked up on my enthusiasm, both for the place and the job. The next thing I knew, he called me for a meeting during which he offered me the job that I had shown interest in and would love to do. I had no experience in guest house management, but that was not going to stand in my way. I had a background of business administration though, which I thought would help although it might not be sufficient. So I suggested to Peter that I would go back to Bedford and enrol on a guest house management course at the local college. It was also agreed that in six months' time I would return and take up the manager's post. I returned to Bedford full of project enthusiasm and a purpose. I loved the six-month course, but it was hard work studying after so many years of being at work. Besides, the teaching methods used in England were more hands-on, completely foreign to me after my studies in the Middle East which involved memorising information and sitting for exams. I was reassured that I was on the right path when I passed with flying colours! The course covered all aspects of the hospitality industry: front office and back office operations, as well as kitchen, health and safety, cooking and dining procedures. The only problem was that these procedures were very appropriate for England but not well adapted to East Jerusalem, an occupied city.

8

Return to a War Zone

JERUSALEM, ISRAEL – 1991

I completed the six-month course in December 1990. The Gulf War was on, and I was getting ready to take up my post in Jerusalem. The unfolding drama and intensifying rumours of an Iraqi Scud missile attack on Jerusalem prompted family and friends to share their horror when they heard that I was still planning to go:

'Are you mad? People are leaving Jerusalem and you want to go there?' they said.

That fell on deaf ears – I was ready. In my pocket I had two precious pieces of paper: my guest house certificate, proof of my ability to do the work, and my British passport, allowing me to enter and live in Jerusalem. Now there were no more restrictions on entering the country of my birth; no need for a visa, no more waiting at embassies to get one, no more uncertainty about getting permission stamped in my passport. But the most important aspect of having the British passport was that now I belonged somewhere on this vast Planet Earth, and I was not a refugee. My joy at becoming a subject of a country, and a great country at that, increased my self-confidence.

The one place I desperately wanted to visit was Haifa, where I had been born. I wanted a chance to connect with my roots. I was so excited with the prospect of a new place, a new job and a new challenge; it swept me off my feet. Nothing was going to stop me from realising my dream of managing a guest house. God's plan was unfolding, Scud missiles or no Scud missiles.

Although the war was in full swing, amazingly I had a perfect sense of calm, a wonderful peace, an excitement and an assurance that I was doing the right thing. I was not rattled and was so very grateful to my church, especially my friends and my house group, for supporting me in this. As far as my family were concerned, they accepted my decision, although Mother kept her feelings to herself. I was aware that she knew that I had not been happy in my work and that I was searching for that contentment that had eluded me so far. She was also happy for me to find my roots and to connect with the extended family that no one had seen for the past forty-three years.

I bade farewell to family and friends, after putting my affairs in order. *Jerusalem, here I come!* I was looking forward to the unknown, full of hope and trusting the God who had got me to where I was – another step on the stepping stones to belonging and identity?

After a four-hour flight on 10th January 1991, the British Airways plane landed at Ben Gurion airport in Tel Aviv. It was 10 pm on a dreary and cold night. The atmosphere was very tense; not surprising, given that there was a war on and rumours of an imminent Scud missile attack were rife. After a considerable delay, I cleared customs. What a relief to see the cheerful face of Peter, who was waiting for me. After an hour's drive, we arrived at St George's Guest House.

I spent the first hectic days familiarising myself with my surroundings and was introduced to staff, volunteers, clergy, the bishop and everyone else who had a connection with the cathedral. But lurking in the background, intense preparations were in full swing for a shelter against the gas Scud missiles. A bathroom was chosen as a safe room, with all windows sealed and darkened, and everyone in the compound was issued with a gas mask.

Sunday, 18th January 1991, at 10 pm, the rumours became a reality: the sirens shrieked and wailed, shattering the serenity and quietness of the cathedral. I grabbed my gas mask and my coat, and scurried in my slippers to the Scud missile shelter in the next building. Ten of us sat huddled together, hiding behind protruding eyes and long snout masks, a picture of shadowy aliens from another planet.

Welcome to the Holy Land! Welcome to the land of my birth! What have I done? Was coming the right decision?

We sat on the bathroom's cold floor in darkness and mumbled, talking to each other through the gas masks. We waited and waited, apprehension mounting for the Scud missiles to hit. Three hours passed. They never did. The sirens wailed again, releasing us from the bathroom shelter. That night, Saddam Hussein's missiles reached Tel Aviv and Haifa but missed Jerusalem. We were spared and very grateful to God, but it was a fearful introduction to my new job. Would life continue to be like this? Then I remembered all the events that had led me to this place and was reassured by the continued peace I had had since I had decided to take on this job.

One morning, soon after I arrived, I walked down Salaheddin Street, towards the Old City, passing the Garden Tomb on my left. Men dressed in long, baggy pants and colourful *keffiyehs* briskly overtook me, rushing to attend Friday prayers at Al Aqsa Mosque on Temple Mount. I entered the Old City through a huge stone gate flanked by two turrets. I stared in front of me as if in a daze, as I pictured the invading armies noisily marching through the narrow cobbled streets. When they passed, I saw in my imagination a gentle person following slowly behind, jostled by the crowds, weary with a heavy cross on His back. He walked the Via Dolorosa – the Way of the Cross.

I was soon brought back to reality by the pushing and shoving of the crowds around me, and the spell of those faraway times receded. I continued slowly, manoeuvring my steps through the narrow streets stretching in all directions, savouring the myriad smells of spices and fruits, and taking in the sights and noises of the unique city. I had entered the bustling bazaars and shops of the Palestinian Quarter.

All that I saw and heard was not confined to the Old City alone. As on the Friday morning, the Muezzin from the top of the minaret at a local mosque called the faithful to prayer, while on late Friday afternoon the sirens wailed and shrieked again, not warning of an imminent Scud missile but to notify people to observe the start of *Shabbat*, the Sabbath day. When Sunday came, the bells of St George's Cathedral called all Christians to worship. It did not matter if you were a Palestinian, British, American Christian or any other Christian pilgrim, all were welcome. My spirits lifted as I joined the cathedral choir in singing and praising God. For a short hour, all the conflicts outside the cathedral walls between the ethnic and religious groups were forgotten, and peace and tranquillity reigned.

St George's Cathedral is part of the three monotheistic religions that dominate Old Jerusalem's make-up. The proximity of Christian, Islamic and Jewish sites to each other is astonishing. Actually, the sites are only a few miles apart: the Holy Sepulchre, the Dome of the Rock and the Wailing Wall, among others. Beyond the cathedral walls, to the east, lies the Muslim majority and minority Christian-occupied East Jerusalem, a Palestinian enclave. To the west and beyond the main highway lie Mea Shearim, the Haredim Orthodox Jewish enclave and West Jerusalem.

Although Islam and Judaism are miles apart in terms of theology, I could not help but notice the underlying similarities in the practices of both ethnic groups. Halal meat intake on one side matched kosher food on the other; one group wore head-dresses and long flowing robes, the other wigs, hats and heavy, thick, long coats – even in summer. On Fridays the Muezzin called the faithful to the mosques and in the evenings sirens called all the faithful to observe *Shabbat*. They are so close, yet so far apart.

Inside St George's close walls it was a different story. The Cathedral Close was now my new home, and I had a nice small flat at one end of the compound. I was part of the guest house, which had twenty-four rooms with facilities. The British dean was responsible for all the cathedral's affairs, together with St George's Guest House, which employed both Christian and Muslim staff. The British Anglican Church had been the custodians of the cathedral since 1898. The Palestinian bishop shared the cathedral with the British as the seat of the Palestinian Anglican diocese, serving the whole of the Middle East. The bishop's house, part of the diocese, occupied the centre of the Close. That left, at the far end of the premises, the American Presbyterian College, run by an American clergyman. They offered biblical courses all year round in their newly built college in the Close.

The Palestinians, British and Americans shared this amazing close. Added to this mix, we were blessed with many volunteers from all over the world, who contributed richly to the special atmosphere there, with its unique, diverse make-up of people. Very vibrant discussion topics, religious or political, were not in short supply, and took place at mealtimes between laymen and clergy.

These special mealtimes were not to be missed, as college students joined staff, guests, visitors and pilgrims at the table. The kitchen cooks and dining room staff were very busy on a daily basis catering – providing and serving delicious Palestinian meals for up to ninety at any one sitting. The dynamics of running a twenty-four-bed guest house were more than a full-time job. Working with so many interesting, diverse people of many different backgrounds, languages, nationalities and cultures, both local and foreign, added another great dimension to the dizzyingly charged atmosphere around me.

To add to this melee of wonderful people that one met at St George's, I must mention 'Jerusalem Syndrome'. I am not sure if you are familiar with the term, so in case you are not, I will explain.

I received a call from the American consulate in East Jerusalem one morning, asking if I had accommodation for an American citizen at the guest house.

'Yes, I have one room for a longer stay than a week,' I answered.

'We are not sure how long he will stay with you, but we would like him to be on full board. We are in the process of repatriating him to the US.'

'What is his name?' I asked expectantly

'Well, he calls himself Elijah [i.e. the prophet Elijah]; we are really not sure who he is at this stage,' he added.

Jerusalem Syndrome afflicted some tourists who came with highly charged religious expectations and beliefs. When they landed in the 'holy city', saw all its holy landmarks and then saw the unholy reality on the ground, they ended up spiritually and emotionally confused, suffering from an identity crisis. We had many bizarre conversations with the 'prophet Elijah' over meals.

To safeguard my sanity, I escaped for well-deserved coffee breaks with a few volunteers to the American Colony hotel down the road, the home of many a journalist who covered the news from the Palestinian East Jerusalem. We constantly needed to remind ourselves that there was a world outside the Close's intense, protective walls.

Having said that, the joy of being there, upheld by the prayers of my home church and doing what I loved and was meant to be doing, energised me every morning. I woke up refreshed and excited. Making my way along the long corridor from my flat down to the sunny gardens below, I passed fragrant spring flower beds and the delicious pomelo-laden tree, chatted to visitors as I passed and looked forward to the challenges that the day would bring. I loved the work, which had all the ingredients that had been missing in all my other jobs except my work with students in Beirut. Some of the challenges we faced were unsurmountable; still, it provided me with the satisfaction I craved for. I had found my vocation at last, as I naturally met, greeted and interacted with guests, visitors and pilgrims. I reverted to the trait of hospitality that every Middle Eastern person possesses and it felt very comfortable.

Getting to grips with the intricate workings of the guest house in a 'foreign' land, answering to three bosses, was sometimes more than challenging though. My first responsibility was to the cathedral dean and the guest house. Through Peter, the dean, I was next answerable to the Palestinian bishop, who had the overall responsibility of the Anglican diocese seat in the Middle East. Lastly, I had to answer to the college dean, because the guest house catered to all their students' meals.

I learnt to adjust quickly. This was no ordinary place. Inside the walls I worked with different cultures and nationalities, contrary to the cruel reality outside of the walls in which there was a crushing, unjust treatment of Palestinians by the occupying forces. Day by day, the heavy weight of an oppressive occupation became increasingly apparent to me. The fifteen or so guest house Palestinian staff came from the Old City and the neighbourhood villages of Silwan and Abu Dis, a mile or two from the Old City. They were dedicated to their jobs but were often unable to turn up for work, as the special passes from the occupying authorities were meagrely given and mostly refused. The only route open to them was by walking miles over hills and clambering round hamlets to avoid the Israeli checkpoints. A journey that would otherwise have taken twenty minutes took them hours. The pressures of not being able to get to work, together with the undignified sufferings of being searched and made to feel they were foreigners in their inherited land, was sometimes too much to bear.

Although I spoke the language, everything about the country, the job and the people was new to me. I had enthusiasm and energy – maybe too much. This was my birthplace but a country which I did not know. I realised that I had come a long way from being a Middle Easterner, especially as I had adopted and was happy in my newly acquired culture.

Looking back, I think I would have saved myself times of bewilderment and anxiety if I had gone there better equipped with people management skills. My problem was that I expected from everyone else what I expected from myself: dedication. Some rose to the challenge, like the young cook who wanted to get somewhere in life, but not the head waiter, who had seen it all and was comfortable with how things were and didn't want any change. He couldn't adjust to the management shift from a British manager to a female Palestinian one. In his view, and as far as he was concerned, I was a Middle Easterner; he could not understand and was disappointed when I adhered to my new British culture and acted accordingly. I was stranded between two camps; I understood them both, but fell short by not being able to bridge the cultural gap between them.

I also appreciated what the staff went through as they lived under the tyrannical misery of the occupation. The tensions climbed over the guest house walls from the streets; how many times did I see young Palestinians being humiliated and abused for no other specific reason than that they were Palestinians?

One Sunday, Israeli soldiers stormed the closed iron gates of the compound's thick walls, looking for the bishop. I was disturbed and frightened as they came in with their machine guns.

'Israeli occupying soldiers are not allowed into a Jerusalem religious place,' Peter told me.

The bishop was away that day.

Inside as well as outside the Close we had challenges. A Palestinian worker was electrocuted during renovations works. While the paramedics desperately tried to save his life, I rushed to the cathedral in tears and, on my knees, I pleaded with God to save his life. That was not to be. I was heartbroken, and the grief shook me to the core, bringing me very close to the end of my endurance.

On the other hand, there were positive and rewarding aspects of the job. A few months in, I had control of the guest house finances, and our books showed full reservations for months ahead. Our financial situation was in a very healthy position with a surplus, indicating that for the first time, we were able to buy the guest house's own car. It made running the guest house much more smooth and efficient, and gave us the added freedom of being able to drive out to discover the countryside. I enjoyed so much driving with some of our volunteers, through the undisturbed countryside to the Cistercian Latrun Monastery, renowned for its special vineyards. We bought our monthly wine requirements after spending time chatting to the monks and tasting their wines. We had great times exploring the beautiful countryside steeped in our Christian faith, reminding me that these hamlets, hills and lakes had not changed for over two thousand years; they were the same ones that our Lord Jesus walked on and preached from.

One day, I drove for the first time with friends towards Tiberius from Nazareth. It was a bright sunny day, and at midday the sun started to burn instead of shine. I drove slowly as I approached the steep descent into the town, when a huge, pearl-shaped, shimmering lake suddenly appeared in the distance. A sea of glass was in front of our eyes and it took our breath away: a freshwater lake, 215 metres below sea level, nestled and surrounded by hills. In front of us was the most beautiful sight I had seen for a long time, the Sea of Galilee – a place I would one day return to again.

I also had wonderful times visiting and being heartily welcomed by members of my father's and mother's extended families in Nazareth and Haifa. It warmed my heart to get to know uncles, aunts and cousins that I had only known by name. It was such a pleasure to be part of this wonderful extended family. What a joy – here I was, for the first time in forty-four years, sitting with them chatting over delicious Palestinian meals.

Another drive that brought me special pleasure was a trip south with friends. We drove twenty miles out of Jerusalem, through the barren Judean sandy hills towards the Dead Sea, stopping at Wadi (valley) Kelt. From the roadside we looked around and could only see wilderness surrounding us. Then, at the bottom of the Wadi, we spotted St George's Monastery, nestling in, and clinging precariously to, the edges of the ravine's cliffs.

The only way to reach the monastery was to get on a donkey or go on foot, so I opted for the donkey ride as the descent was so steep. One step forward, two steps backwards on the snaking dirt paths, our puny donkeys slipped and stumbled but made it slowly down the bare hills. It was scary, and I held the stumbling donkey's bridle for dear life. A sigh of relief escaped my lips when I made it all the way down without falling off. But what a place when I saw it in front of me! I lifted my eyes to the top of the clinging structure and could not miss the preserved cave where they say that Elijah fled, hid and was fed by ravens.

As we made our way back on our donkeys, the story of the man who fell among thieves came to life for me. The scenery was so evocative of the New Testament account, and the only reminder of a later era was St George's Monastery itself.

Encounters of a different kind

One of the disruptive procedures I had to go through, during the year and a half that I was at St George's, was to leave the country every three months. That was mandatory as I did not have, and could not obtain, a work permit. Each of these exits and returns was as memorable as the next. Despite the passage of years, they are still clear in my memory.

The first three months were up in March 1991, and I flew to the UK on my first compulsory week's holiday. It was a good break and I returned with many items and furnishings to enhance the décor of the guest rooms. The plane landed at 4 am, and I was prepared for the usual intimidating grilling, designed to make one cringe. The security officer looked at me briefly, then she fired these question at me in succession:

'Why are you in Jerusalem?'

'Who are you going to see?'

'Who do you know?'

Then, genuinely puzzled, and looking at my British passport, she asked:

'Why aren't you carrying an Israeli passport, since you were born in Haifa?'

She was young and I understood her predicament: I guess her historical knowledge did not go back forty-three years to the time when the land in question had been called Palestine. I had arrived at a place which was part of me. I had been born here, yet deep down in my heart, I knew she did not want to acknowledge or accept who I was. Her denial did not change the fact that I had been born in Haifa, a Christian Palestinian, and not an Israeli Jew. This denial intimidated and created anxiety and disquiet in me. What was more, I did not know Hebrew. But detecting some Arabic words in the conversations, I remembered where I was going to work: I would be in the Arab sector of the city, among people I loved and belonged to. It calmed my fears, anxieties and nerves.

That was stressful enough, but I was not prepared for what came next, which was even more distressing than the questioning. The unfolding drama shocked me. My suitcases were shoved onto the big X-ray machine, and immediately a shrill alarm sounded loudly and lights flashed all over the airport and did not stop. To make things worse, very agitated security staff and soldiers ran in all directions, shouting and barking orders in Hebrew, pointing to the doors of the arrival hall. They screamed, 'צא החוצה'

Not understanding what they were saying but getting the gist of their orders, I followed everyone out, wondering what the problem was. In no time, the big arrival hall was deserted. Half an hour later, we were ushered back in. I went to retrieve my suitcases that were still on the X-ray machine and I noticed the screen displaying what was inside my suitcase: wire coils. The penny dropped – ah, that was what they spotted in my suitcase and thought it was a bomb; that was what triggered the alarm. Hence the complete evacuation of the arrival hall! My suitcases were the culprits; they had three wire-coiled lampshades in them (the collapsible type). I had bought these in the UK for the guest house bedrooms. 'Welcome to Jerusalem!' I chuckled.

Mother came to visit me in Jerusalem halfway through my time there and I met her at the airport. She had a special entry visa in her passport that Uncle Emile, a Knesset MP, had been able to arrange for her. Now in her eighties, she arrived back after fifty years of forced absence, and certainly not a willing one, from her birthplace, Shefa-Amr near Nazareth. She had become a refugee, first to Lebanon and then to the UK. After she cleared customs, I met her, but instead of meeting the waiting family outside, we were both led to an interrogation room. The joy of being on home soil again was marred by an hour of questioning. The young soldier went on and on, questioning her about who she was and who she knew in the country, and so on. Although they recognised her brother as an MP in the Knesset, it did not make any difference. As the interrogation didn't seem to come to an end, I noticed that Mother was getting fidgety and her patience was running thin. Suddenly, she got up, looked squarely at her interrogator, and interrupted him in mid-sentence:

'You are a Jew?'

Then, before he even had time to answer yes, she continued:

'God bless you!'

And with that, she marched across the room in a hurry, her handbag dangling on her arm, before going out through the open door. Mother dismissed herself without a backward look. I followed quickly, looking apologetically at the officer. The man looked vaguely bemused, but did not say a word and let us go.

During our precious time together, we spent great times visiting relatives, retracing Mother's steps and memories to places she remembered as a child, as a young woman living with her parents, seven brothers and only sister, and later on as a mother of four girls. The most memorable of these was when we went up the stony steps to *Flat 13a*, our last home in Haifa before we became refugees, on Abbas Street, on Mount Carmel and just below the Bahai Gardens. We knocked on the door and the occupant, a Jewish woman, asked what we wanted. Mother explained that she wished to show me where I was born. The woman was kind enough and let us in. Mother went round the flat from room to room, showing me where I had been born and the position of the cot I had slept in as a baby. She also pointed out the occupants of the other floors, my grandparents and one of her brothers who had owned the building. This physical, tangible existence of my birthplace strengthened my acceptance of where my roots were and who I was.

Another period of three months passed; my visa expired, and it was again time to leave and return. It was a freezing cold morning when I checked in at the airport for the London flight, exhausted but looking forward to getting home and resting. But before that, I had to endure the dreaded heavy-handed official harassment, just because I had a Palestinian name. My British passport did not help or shield me. The inevitable questioning and rigorous searching began; the contents of my suitcase were out for all to see – the good, the bad and the ugly. The Israeli female custom officer frisked me thoroughly.

'Take off your boots,' she then demanded. (In those days, Israel was the only country to ask travellers to take off their shoes to examine them, before it was adopted internationally.)

I was so exhausted, desperate and angry by then that, without thinking, I blurted out:

'I have put these boots on early this morning and I don't intend to take them off now.'

'Take them off,' she repeated.

'If you want my boots off, you have to do it yourself.' I raised my boot towards her.

She reached down and took them off, checked there was nothing in them and gave them back to me. Silently, I put them back on, but time was ticking on and my ordeal was not over yet. Next she targeted my hairdryer, taking it away to examine it. It was returned to me, having obviously been dismantled, and I was supposed to put it back in my suitcase. I looked at her in disbelief:

'Do you expect me to accept this? You took a perfectly functioning hairdryer from my suitcase and you have returned a dysfunctional one. I am not leaving this airport until you fix my hairdryer,' I stated confidently, knowing that carrying a British passport gave me the edge in this situation.

She disappeared with the ruined hairdryer, and a quarter of an hour later came back with a £20 note, enough to buy me a new one in those days. I thanked her and scrambled to get on the plane just in time for take-off.

Bright interlude

We needed something to lift our spirits at this time in Jerusalem, and what better than the visit of the Archbishop of Canterbury, George

Carey, to bless the diocese? The diocese invited two hundred notable Jerusalem guests to meet and have lunch with him after the Sunday service. As the manager of the guest house, I was responsible (with my cooks and dining room staff) for this great occasion. Everything was ready, the guests were all there, the cooks produced a Palestinian feast for the occasion and it was hot and ready to be served, but the archbishop was nowhere to be seen. The plan was that he would come by car from Amman, Jordan to Israel. But unfortunately, this was the first Easter in many years that Jerusalem lay under snow in April. It snowed heavily for days, and all roads were completely impassable as they were blocked by snow. The Jordanian / Israeli River Jordan border crossing was flooded. Three hours late, the archbishop arrived by limousine. On one of my trips manoeuvring the icy distance (30m) between the kitchen and dining rooms, supervising lunch preparations, I fell on the slippery ice. I am glad to say that I did not break any of my bones, but my limbs ached for a week afterwards. It was a small incident if I compare it to the great occasion of meeting and hosting the archbishop at the guest house.

Easter Sunday was such a special day as we gathered at the Via Dolorosa, the Way of the Cross, with the Bishop of Jerusalem, together with many others, including a host of clergy and Christian pilgrims from all over the world. The atmosphere was emotionally and spiritually charged as we marched. Then at each of the fourteen stations, the flowing mass of black robes that crammed the old, narrow cobbled streets to bursting stopped. At each station one member of the clergy read the narrative from the Gospels and prayed under a cloudless sky. When finished, each Christian denomination (and there were quite a few) moved on to the next station, behind their own banner and cross. At this point, curious shop owners came out of their small shops to view the yearly procession. I was thankful as it was more than just a procession for me; as I walked, I realised that the narrow street I was on was the same dirt alleyway Jesus had walked through carrying the heavy cross on his shoulder, making his way to Golgotha and to his crucifixion, where He made the ultimate sacrifice and paid with his death to release me from my heavy burdens.

What a tangible confirmation of my Christian faith!

Jewish literary prize

What a privilege! Emile Habiby, Mother's brother, well known author and a member of the Knesset, invited me to his Arabic literary prize-giving ceremony on 7th May 1992. It was the highest, most prestigious literary prize that the Jewish State gave to any deserving writer. His humorous, satirical writings about Palestinians who stayed behind in Palestine after the establishment of the Jewish State were viewed by some Israelis as promoting coexistence between the two communities, while they were viewed by some Palestinians as a betrayal. I joined his family as we made our way across the divided city from Arab East Jerusalem to the Convention Centre in Jewish West Jerusalem. I was overcome by trepidation and apprehension; being a Palestinian living in the East part of Jerusalem, I had never been in the Jewish part of the city before – it was a no-go area for me emotionally, mentally and physically. On entering the big auditorium, my nervousness and fear reached a high pitch; the Hebrew chatter was very loud. I felt a stranger and out of place, but took comfort from the fact that I was sitting next to my relatives; this calmed my nerves a little, but I couldn't help thinking to myself:

This huge auditorium is full of people I can hardly trust. Didn't they leave me homeless, searching for both a home and an identity? What am I doing among them? How can Uncle accept a prize from them? Is his memory so short, has he forgotten what they did to all of us – made us refugees?

These negative thoughts flashed through my mind, but immediately I reminded myself that in acceptance and forgiveness lay my peace. I had forgiven those who had harmed us and, by doing so, I had freed myself of bitterness and anger.

My reverie was interrupted by the audience clapping when the literary prize nominees, winners and all the dignitaries filed in one by one and sat down on the comfortable semicircular stage chairs. The clapping reached crescendo levels as Yitzhak Shamir, the prime minister, and the president followed last and sat down.

Proceedings started, speech after speech, and of course it was all in Hebrew. I was able to glean one word here and one word there that sounded like Arabic, but did not understand anything of substance.

The controversy that had divided both the Jewish and Palestinian camps, as I understood it, was this. Emile Habiby was an Arab, and this was a Jewish literary prize. By conferring it on an Arab, it meant Israel's acknowledgement of the Palestinian Arabs amongst them, which they had been trying very hard to suppress. On the Arab side, accepting it from an occupier meant an outright betrayal of all the Palestinians' rights and aspirations. Uncle's thinking, as I understood it, had been captured in his answer when I had I asked him earlier if he would shake Shamir's hand at the prize-giving ceremony:

'If he wants to shake my hand, I would gladly shake his,' was his reply.

The speeches were over, then nominees' names were called out, and one by one they got up from their chairs and received their prizes from the prime minister while the audience continued clapping. Then...

'Emile Habiby.'

A great hush descended on the auditorium. Uncle Emile slowly got up from his chair and took a few measured steps in his distinctive way, which brought him face to face with the prime minister and his outstretched hand. They looked at each other and then vigorously shook hands. Instantaneously, cheering and clapping erupted, and the entire audience got to its feet in a standing ovation. Immediately, however, loud shouts and a commotion came from the front row. Then I saw three big men ushering out of the hall a yelling man who was loudly protesting and shouting in Hebrew. Later I learnt that he was a previous Jewish winner, objecting to the prize going to a Palestinian / Israeli Arab.

Uncle Emile was greatly respected by prominent literary and political people, both Palestinian and Jewish. By being the representative of the Arab Communist party at the Knesset, he had a wide contact base. I attended a few occasions with him when he had meetings speaking in Arabic or English; I was always spellbound by his delivery, charisma and mastery of the Arabic literary language. His published books are his legacy. I was really amazed the first time I heard him speak, together with Edward Said, the Palestinian / American academic, at a meeting in London some years ago.

It was a real privilege to belong to the Habiby and Musallam clans, as it was also a joy to meet so many of them, but on many occasions I lost track of who was who, and who was related to whom, and in which order!

A changing situation

At the end of nineteen months being the manager of St George's Guest House, I found that no two days had been the same. There were many great and rewarding times to offset the political stresses and the demanding work. I lived and enjoyed my life to the full with the small cathedral 'family' – the memorable trips we made together to Masada and Ein Gedi; a silent retreat in a monastery; the joy of being part of the cathedral choir worshipping together on Sundays; the precious time I spent with many visiting friends, with the countless wet dips we took together in the Dead Sea's dark grey mud; the solitary moments I spent praying at the Garden Tomb, a few minutes' walk from the guest house. My life was deeply enriched by meeting and getting to know so many people from all over the world. It was a vibrant, amazing existence, and I found myself and my vocation through a rewarding profession.

We were a hard-working team at the guest house; nevertheless, when Peter left, I was devastated, bereft of his support and of his cheerful and encouraging personality. I loved it when he called me Fifi. The place was never the same when it lost its anchor.

No wonder, when the summer days were upon us, that I became increasingly anxious, stressed and very tired. I knew I could not maintain the successful level of managing the guest house, given the major stresses both outside and inside the walls. The responsibilities affected my health, and at the end of the day I suffered, unable to continue with the challenging pressures that the guest house presented. I loved the work and I put into it all that God had given me. But that was not enough as my physical, mental, emotional and spiritual well-being was eroded; I was completely drained.

The time for my summer vacation was upon me. I was looking forward so much to going home for the summer months, especially as the kitchen and guest rooms refurbishment programme was underway with no guests expected. That wasn't to be, however; the bishop had other ideas and asked me to stay on and oversee the work. I was overwhelmed and devastated, for that kind of work was not in my contract. It was the straw that broke the camel's back, and I resigned in June 1992.

Was the whole experience worth it despite the difficulties? Yes, every minute of it, for three reasons.

Firstly, I enjoyed and was able to do the work that the Lord wanted me to do, despite the challenges and difficulties. My Christian faith grew tangibly stronger as I relied on him. Being there physically, and having walked on the same ground that Jesus walked on, my faith came alive. I gained a new dimension to my understanding of the Scriptures, the basis of my faith.

Secondly, it helped me acknowledge to myself who I was, and assured me there was no shame in being born a Palestinian as the world had made me believe. My roots belonged with this wonderful extended family in the country of my birth.

Thirdly, managing the day-to-day activities of the guest house gave me so much pleasure. It also helped me gain confidence at the end, knowing that I had successfully fulfilled all my obligations and contract. The greatest joy was associating with, and getting to know, people who enriched my life.

9

The Scottish Guest House

TIBERIUS, ISRAEL – 1993

I was back in Bedford on 1st July 1992, with time to reflect on the unique time and experience I had had in Jerusalem, a year and a half of lows and highs. But it was not for long, because at the end of the month, I received an invitation to manage the Scottish Sea of Galilee Guest House (the 'Scottie'), in Tiberius, North Israel. Evidently, the Episcopal Church were pleased with what I had accomplished in Jerusalem. Like at St George's, the Scottish Guest House was moving from the Scottish church's jurisdiction into the local church's. Their management team, up to then, was made up of a Scottish manager with four volunteers, a Palestinian cook with four dining-room staff and five Jewish room-service employees. The combination of the staff ethnicity mix should have alerted me to the difficulties ahead.

I accepted the invitation, and in January 1993 I arrived in Tiberius. Immediately, I was issued with a work permit as the manager of the guest house in the Jewish state. I attempted to learn Hebrew, but without success, partly due to my workload and partly due to an uncomfortable feeling of betrayal of my Palestinian heritage. Added to this, I was still bearing the emotional aftermath of my experience in Jerusalem. I did not feel at ease with the different nationalities of volunteers and paid staff, as they did not get on together. Also, I was not able to adjust and cope with the staff's strong temperaments and entrenched attitudes. Both town and guest house were oppressive places to work in. Temperatures soared up to the thirties and forties in summer, with air conditioning only in the two newly refurbished guest-buildings but not in the remaining three. Although English, Arabic and Hebrew were spoken at the guest house, Hebrew was the official language, therefore making my job more complicated as I did not possess it. An added emotional difficulty I faced was that both Tiberius and Safad bore the identity of previously owned

Palestinian towns more than any other place I had seen; this cruel and sad reminder only increased my stress.

In hindsight, taking the Tiberius job at such short notice, and not giving myself enough time to regain strength, proved costly. Here again, I was in a completely new situation, with more difficult challenges than in Jerusalem. There the atmosphere was vibrant and full of life, while here it was gloomy and lifeless. Nevertheless, the encouragement of the many friends who came to visit me during this time kept me going, restoring my flagging spirits.

Our neighbours, the American nuns who lived just up the road from the 'Scottie', became friends, and I would often visit them. I appreciated their friendship, which developed as we went to Hebrew lessons together attempting to learn the language. One day, they came to see me carrying a bundle. I was delighted when they gave me a fluffy puppy.

'Where did you get it from?' I asked, surprised.

'Oh, well, we just picked it up from the street in downtown Tiberius. We found him roaming with other dogs. We are sure he will give you a lot of joy,' they said.

'No owners?' I queried.

'Not really. Maybe at one time in their brief puppyhood lives they were cherished gifts to young men and women. But soon afterwards, they lost their status and homes when their owners were drafted into the army and they were left on the streets,' they explained.

Scottie had given me joy at first – he was my shadow and would sit under my chair in the office for hours – but I did not have the skills or the time to train him. At one point, my necklaces disappeared, and after some investigation I found out that he had eaten them all. The joy he was supposed to give me was offset by his unruly, obsessive behaviour later on. I was very relieved when I was able to give him away to a good family looking for a pet.

I was the transitional manager chosen for this period, but I was not the right manager needed to transfer the Scottish management to the local Episcopal hands. This transition did not need a 'foreigner' like me but a local Palestinian / Israeli resident, and there were many who belonged and understood the complicated workings among all the parties. I did not belong and was in no one's camp, so I resigned after a very hard and stressful time.

I survived exactly a year in Tiberius! Having achieved what I thought was the top of where I wanted to be in my career, I returned to Bedford in December 1993. What did I find in Galilee? Absolutely nothing of what I was looking for: no satisfaction, belonging or peace.

Immediately on my return, I joined a counselling course at St John's Extension Studies in Nottingham. For what reason? Not to counsel others, but to sort out and understand some of the 'whys' I had been through. The course was therapeutic and dealt with some issues – but not all.

10

YMCA

BEDFORD, UK – 1994

I had been in this situation before! But now I was ready to face another job and get on with my life. I went to many job interviews, including posts in hotels and bird sanctuaries. In the end, I was offered a deputy manager's job at the YMCA in Bedford. I would not have chosen it, as I did not feel I could make a good transition from a hospitality-oriented guest house to young people's sheltered accommodation. But I was desperate to get back to earning my living and it was the only job on offer. I accepted it, saying to myself that it would be only for few months until I found something better. But that 'better' never happened; the months dragged into years – into precisely *eight* years.

I was nowhere near my goal of belonging, and I was desperate. I had nothing to show for all the hard work and fifty-plus years of existence except heartache, pain and loneliness. These were so unbearable that I resorted to Christian meeting sites on the internet, still in its infancy in those days. I met one Christian from one such site a few times, but the old fears surfaced, together with my minister's warning 'not to get involved with this gentleman' whom he knew. So after lunch in Bedford one Sunday, we parted company and said goodbye for the last time. Then I took myself off to nearby Stewartby, a disused brick quarry, and cried my eyes out. I was emotionally broken and I couldn't share it with anybody, not even with my mother and my sister's family. I sat in the car with the rain beating heavily on the roof, adding to my gloom and sorrow. After an hour, I drove back home, opened the front door and entered with tears streaming down my face. With a broken heart, I cried out:

'Lord, if you don't come up with me to my lonely flat, I am not going upstairs.'

I rushed upstairs through the house to the top floor, avoiding any member of the family seeing me. Before I reached the last step, a deep sense of calm filled me. The searing grief and pain that was embedded in my heart lifted. It was gone like a plucked thorn; it was no more. I was engulfed by a profound sense of hope, peace and calm.

Now the realisation dawned on me, and I was satisfied, that a committed married life was not the best thing for me. I was able to put my life on the first step to recovery and healing.

11

A Challenging Three Months

IBILLIN, ISRAEL – 1997

I had been working as Deputy Manager at the YMCA in Bedford for a few years now. There was no new job on the horizon and my restless feet kept wanting to move on to something else. I did not tolerate ruts which were not advantageous to fulfilling my goal of finding a sense of belonging.

I had got to know Father Elias Chacour, founder of Mar Elias College in Ibillin, Israel and author of *Blood Brothers*, when I was in Jerusalem in 1992. I introduced him to Peter and Gill, my pastor and his wife, when they came to visit me there. They forged a deep and strong friendship that promoted Palestinian understanding in Bedford and the UK through the establishment of the 'Elijah Trust' charity. Gill dedicated her life, time and energy to the charity. My indebtedness is recorded here to Gill, Peter, all the trustees, volunteers and all who were involved in and supported the Elijah Trust, for all their hard work and dedication during the fifteen years of the trust's life. My gratitude goes much deeper, as they were instrumental in helping me with the healing process of finding and accepting myself for who I was: a Palestinian Christian.

As a result of what the trust meant to me, I felt compelled to help Father Chacour when he needed a personal assistant in Ibillin. I took leave without pay from my YMCA deputy manager's job and joined the staff at Mar Elias College as a volunteer. I was there for three months, including Christmas 1997. As well as helping Fr Chacour, I was also hoping that I would find, once and for all, whether the land of my birth was where I should settle down.

There, even more than in Jerusalem or Tiberius, I felt I did *not* belong. The culture I had adopted over the past fifteen years had made it too difficult for me to revert back to a culture I had been familiar with when I was younger. This inability allowed me little interaction with the community besides speaking Arabic and enjoying the food, but it was not enough to make me one of them. I think we both contributed to this state of affairs; their Israeli-Arab and my British-Arab identities camouflaged and obscured our original Palestinian roots.

Even in Ibillin, however, without a paying job and an income, the Lord was gracious to me and provided the finances, through gifts, to tide me over during the three months I was there. It was a good break but I was sure, like never before, that that place was not home. Father Chacour tempted me with promises if I would only stay, including an offer of a tour of St Paul's journeys to Europe, but to no avail.

I was nearer my goal now, as I knew who I was, a Christian Palestinian, but I needed a dot on a geographical map to confirm my identity. Which was it going to be: seven and a half years as a Palestinian in Haifa, Palestine / Israel; or the forty years in Lebanon, as a Lebanese; or the most recent, twelve years as a British subject in Bedford, UK? Why was I confused? I concluded that my wandering life, moving from country to country, not being married and settled down with a family, had a lot to do with this state of mind. I realised, too, that fundamentally it was a spiritual hunger and longing to belong that had set me on this long journey. Without that satisfaction, the identity and peace that I craved would never be found. Towards this end, the next chapter of my life became a factor.

12

A Great Vision

BEDFORD, UK – 2001-2015

Jenny and I attended, and were members of, the same church in Bedford: Russell Park Baptist Church. We shared a great vision that the Lord in his great wisdom had blessed us with, the vision of starting a community coffee shop.

The vision began back in 1997 when we were both involved with the Elijah Trust charity, which was supported by our church. After months of reflection, we developed the idea of a Palestinian information centre in Bedford. To achieve our goal, we attended business seminars and workshops that the council put forward to encourage new businesses. Soon afterwards, though, we realised that an information centre was not a viable and realistic venture, but instead we needed to work towards a community coffee shop in the Castle Road area where we lived. The rationale behind it for me was that the Lord had blessed me with so much in every way, so it was now the right time to give back to the community what He had given me in the first place. I would give my service, time and energy to reach out voluntarily to my community. I was a free woman with no family ties, and in a few years' time I would be retired.

The project took off. Every two weeks we met with a Bedford Council member from the Small Business Department, who supported and oversaw our preparations and planning. For months we worked tirelessly, enjoying every minute of producing business plans, feasibility studies, timetables, house-to-house surveys, schedules and a five-year-budget forecast. In relation to this forecast, David, a church elder, reminded us at the time of the ridiculously high number of cheap cups of coffee / tea we would have to sell to make the project viable. This did not put us off, although we still had many missing pieces of the jigsaw. Among these pieces were:

- The coffee shop needed full-time commitment, but how could Jenny and I leave paid employment?
- How was I going to carry on paying my mortgage, since Jenny and I would run the coffee shop as non-salaried directors?
- Where were we going to get the start-up finance from?
- Was there a suitable property available to rent on Castle Road?
- Who would be willing to join us to make this project viable?
- Would the project succeed?

All these questions did not deter us, as we were driven by an inner force of joy, peace and complete trust in God, which propelled us from one phase to the next. Our aim was to create a space, a place where everyone felt at ease, accepted and welcomed to come in as a customer or as a volunteer – in short, to show God's love in action.

The Jaffa Orchard Community Coffee Shop

One year into our project preparations, on 30th December 1998, my mother went to be with the Lord at the age of ninety-one. I was devastated. She had been my only anchor in this world, and by losing her I was shattered emotionally; it was another three years before I came through this deep loss. But God knew my grief and kept me going by focusing me on the vision He had given us.

In providing us with our beautiful shared home on the River Ouse, *32, The Embankment*, the Lord had replaced what Mother and all of us had lost in Haifa. Nevertheless, after seventeen years I had grown progressively weary. My poor legs were very tired from getting me up and down my flat, two flights of stairs at least four times a day. That was not my only issue; at work at the YMCA, I had to manage three floors in my deputy manager's job, going up and down many times a shift. That meant climbing up and coming down hundreds of steps every day. The other issue concerned sharing the property with my sister's family. We had an understanding when we first moved in that as long as Mother was with us, we would keep on the house together. By 2001 this was no longer the case, as Mother had passed away four years earlier, and Ron, my brother-in-law, three years before that.

I knew I needed to move, but where to? Where was I going to get the money to settle my share of the mortgage, or who was going to buy my flat, which was part of the house? I had lots of questions and doubts. How could it be feasible with all these impossibilities? Was it the right time to leave the big house, my home for the past seventeen years? As I was battling with the issue of moving, I was desperate for someone to help guide me to take the right decision. One morning, I was having my quiet time as usual, and mulled over the subject, praying, 'Lord, what do I do? Do I move or not?' The answer did not take long to come.

During the day, I was at my desk looking through a magazine, when a caption jumped out at me: "Don't wait any longer!" It came alive as I read it again and again. The answer was there in front of me; I had no doubt whatsoever that it was my answer and I had to move. But how was I to do that? The nature of our arrangement wasn't straightforward; I owned a percentage of the house and mortgage, and I was responsible for settling my portion if I wanted to sell. There was also the small detail of not having the money to redeem my share! On the other hand, there was no way I could sell my flat on its own as it was an integral part of the whole house. I was the one wanting to move out and not my sister. As far as I was concerned, it was an impossible situation, but not to the Lord who had looked after me all these past years.

All the above stumbling blocks did not hinder us in our project preparations; on the contrary, we made steady progress. For me, the assurance that I was right to consider moving came in the form of a generous gift from a friend, who released me from the outstanding mortgage. My move was a step closer. What an answer to our prayers!

Next, though: who was to buy my flat? The answer came when my nephew Howard and his family offered to do so. That settled the issue. I was delighted with the outcome. So after seventeen years in the big house, I moved to my own small place in nearby Dudley Street in October 2001.

A big part of the jigsaw was in place, but there was still another important piece to fit in. In order to run the project, both Jenny and I needed to be free from our employment. This same year, 2001, I was one year short of retirement at sixty, according to the mistaken date of birth of 1943. According to my actual birth certificate, however, I was born in 1942, which meant I could retire and start my pension in 2001 instead of a year later. God, in his wisdom and planning, foresaw the timing of my retirement. I resigned from my deputy manager's job at the YMCA with six months still to go to my sixtieth birthday.

Miracles continued to happen. Jenny was given the opportunity to retire early if she wanted to. After many years of dedicated teaching, she retired early that same year. It was the perfect timing! We were both free now to pursue the project in its next stages.

In early 2001, we prepared and executed each phase of our project according to our schedules and planner. But there were still three important missing pieces.

We needed to move a step further and find the team to run the project with us. A big project like that needed heads, feet and hands to make it work. Friends had reminded me time and time again of the time when we had welcomed Mandy and Lorna, friends from church, to my top floor flat on the Embankment, before I moved. We invited them to join us as directors of the project. They accepted willingly, knowing that it was not a salaried appointment. We were all volunteers with one aim: opening the Community Coffee Shop in our retirement to serve our community and our Lord. We were very pleased to have Mandy on board; although she was employed full time, she gave her time, her accounting and her catering expertise to the project. The initial team of directors was in place.

The search for the second piece of the jigsaw, suitable premises, was on. We looked at three sites, but none were suitable for a coffee shop until, one spring day in 2001, Jenny and I stood outside her garage (opposite her house) having a garage sale to raise funds for the forthcoming coffee shop. The sun was shining on the building next to her house. Downstairs it was a video shop with a large patio in front, and upstairs were the offices of a local solicitor. I turned to Jenny.

'Wouldn't it be great if God gave us this wonderful place for our coffee shop? It would be ideal, especially in summer with the patio!' I declared.

A few weeks later, Jenny surprised us with great news: she had seen people moving furniture from the solicitor's offices upstairs. Not wasting any time, she went and spoke to the owner and found out that he was moving and wanted to rent out the offices. 'By the way, the video shop downstairs also want to terminate their lease,' he had added. When she learnt that the whole building was available to rent, she asked him to give her first refusal when he put it on the market and he was happy to do so.

No mistake, the Lord had answered our prayers. These were the same premises we had asked God for that spring day. We rented the building for a seven-year period.

At this stage, two more directors joined us. It was one Sunday after church when Stephen, an elder in our church, approached me.

'Helen and I would love to join you and be part of the project,' he said.

So the start-up board of directors consisted of Stephen, Helen, Lorna, Mandy, Jenny and me. Later on, Vee and Sue joined us.

The last part of the jigsaw was funding. Our bank balance now had enough in it to enable us to start renovations and change the premises into a coffee shop. All the start-up fund was donated by the directors, by the many friends who gave so generously in one way or another, and by some community funding from the council. All these contributions combined brought the project to fruition.

All was in place now: the team, the premises and the funding to start work in earnest.

It took us few months and a lot of hard work and organisation at an initial cost of approximately £25,000 to convert the space into a coffee shop equipped with a kitchen and other facilities. We had to comply with all the council's rules and regulations concerning health and safety in regard to the food industry. We attended a hygiene course at Bedford College. Fire regulations were a big issue in the building, but these were satisfied before we opened up for business. Each of the six directors was responsible for one aspect of the business. We employed one cook but were joined by an army of volunteers. Our status was a registered company and not a charity; that meant we were liable to pay VAT.

The Jaffa Orchard Community Cafe and Gift Shop was opened officially on 2nd August, 2002 by our local MP. On the first day we opened for business, I stood at nine o'clock looking out of the small window overlooking the patio and wondered, *Will anyone come in?*

I shouldn't have worried; the 'Jaffa' was a great success from the word go. It was God's will in the first place, sustained by the prayers of many in our church and beyond. Prices were low, attracting many, and best of all, the place had the warmth and energy of a vibrant hub. It was a place for making friends and meeting people. By serving others, we served Him and showed His love, which was there to be seen by all. Above all, whoever came in was drawn by the mere fact that we were volunteers working hard serving them and at the same time really enjoying our work. We did not want anything in return except to see people happy and looked after. The love and care shown by all the directors to everyone was amazing. Besides all this, it was a great place for around a hundred community volunteers – some trying to find their feet in a working environment or brought to us by social services. Still others joined because, like us, they wanted to give to the community. Very good food, reasonable prices, coupled with a warm welcome and a loving atmosphere was the greatest recipe for many to come in and contribute to the success of the venture! It was for the community, by the community, to the community. All the above resulted in the amazing popularity and success of the Jaffa Orchard.

The main downstairs area with the patio outside was the perfect location for our coffee shop. But what about the large area upstairs? Two rooms were allocated to our offices and the third became an Aladdin's cave full of beautiful craft and art items made by local people. This added attraction was Jenny's inspiration from her mother's idea of selling people's crafts, from paintings to small handcrafts. There were around a hundred artists, craftspeople and charities on our books. When these items were sold, a small percentage was charged, but charities were not liable to these deductions.

As regards outgoings, we started with one paid cook on our books, but later on we had to employ another. Our Sandra was a rock; she was always there after hours keeping the premises clean. She did this for many years, before we got paid cleaners in. Our financial situation was healthy, but in one instance was aided by a contribution from an unexpected source. We had a free water supply for thirty-six months from a non-existent water meter. We started paying for our water supply when we had a meter fitted.

From the start, the centre became a hub of thriving activities: computer training, group badminton and trips, among many others. It was clear from the beginning that Jenny was the energy hub of the project; her enthusiasm and excellent management were infectious. All the directors contributed generously to the project in their special fields, whether it was dedication of their time, service, expertise or material donations.

You ask me why the name 'Jaffa'? It was Jenny's idea – take the J from Jenny, scramble my name, Afaf, put them together and you get Jaffa. The 'Orchard' was added on. Mary, one of our friends, later suggested that Jaffa could stand for 'Jesus, A Friend For All'. It became our motto.

By now, the coffee shop had been in full swing for two years. That was when I started experiencing debilitating headaches that few knew about. I did not share this with many, being the introverted character that I am. The demanding work and constant customer interaction, which I loved, would have been 'a walk in the park' if I had not suffered from these headaches. I dreaded the forward signs of the attacks. They were not migraines; I called them 'rheumatic sinusitis headaches'. I visited my doctor many times and went for a head scan but nothing was diagnosed. As I suffered in silence, my daily life was affected as I restricted my activities. Ibuprofen tablets were my companions, always present in my pocket. I took precautions by always wearing a hat, though I detested hats and protected myself by avoiding cold draughts. Wintertime was the worst. These draining headaches turned my joyful days at the Jaffa into miserable ones and drove me to the only place to get help from. I cried to the Lord:

'Lord, you gave us the Jaffa to run, but if you want to keep me working there, you have to take away these debilitating headaches.'

The answer came not as an instant healing, but as a steady process of using 'Olbas Oil decongestant', which was recommended by a friend. Eventually, I was healed completely of these restricting headaches.

During the fifteen years of Jaffa's life, our God helped us meet all our financial obligations; the rent was paid when due, as all the other bills were settled and paid in full and on time. The same God who helped us meet our financial obligations at the Jaffa continued to help me financially. My working years contributing to the pension fund in this country were only nineteen out of the thirty-five needed for a full pension. I was content with my monthly half-pension, which was enough for my daily needs. Being part of the Jaffa, with lots of friendships, compensated for this deficit, despite the lack of a salary. One day, a trusted friend and volunteer at the Jaffa mentioned that the council were offering free water boiler replacements to people with limited incomes. Indeed, my income was very limited! The cost of a new boiler to replace my thirty-year-old one would cost me around £3,000. I applied, and got a new boiler!

Thank you, friend, and thank you, Bedford Council. But above all, thank you, Lord, for continuing to look after me by meeting my needs as you have done all through these years I have been in the UK.

Besides other means of financial provision that God had opened up for me during this time, I started giving Arabic lessons. Among its many rewards were the joy of teaching it and the many friends I made.

May 2016 arrived. After fifteen years of running a very successful coffee shop, the Jaffa Orchard Company was brought to an end. Many, including me, did not want the facility closed, as it would leave a gaping hole in many people's lives, including mine. However, whichever way you looked at it, we were very tired and could not take on another three-year lease. Both physically and mentally, we were unable to cope with the pressure. Every day that passed as a director after my seventy-third birthday, I was a day older and a day wearier. However, we were able to donate the coffee shop 'lock, stock and barrel' for free to new owners, along with the name. We were delighted and very pleased, for our paramount desire was to keep Jaffa's doors open to its many friends and loyal customers. We left it in their capable hands, prayed and wished them every success.

For the last fifteen years, Jaffa had been my whole life, during which I had experienced the most exciting, wonderful working years despite the challenges of such a busy working environment. What helped me succeed in one and sustained me throughout the other was the continued belief in the strong vision we were given at the beginning: 'serving Him and serving the community'. Besides, these years made my faith grow stronger and helped me become a more mature person.

My reward this side of life was the knowledge that I had followed God's leading, with the added blessing of making so many friends.

One door closes, another opens

An exciting new chapter came into my life to replace the wonderful Jaffa years when they came to an end.

On the day Jaffa closed its doors, I went with Lorna to return the premises' keys to the landlord. It was a miserable, gloomy, rainy May day, but we were both in good spirits. After returning the keys, I came back home, opened my front door, entered the narrow hall and heard myself say loudly these exact words:

'Now, Lord, what do I do; the Jaffa is no more?'

Precisely two days later, amazingly, I received a call from the local Kings Arms Project, asking me if I would help to interpret for the new Syrian refugee families that the government had accepted into the country. It is worth noting here that through my church, Russell Park Baptist Church, I had put my name down to help the Syrian refugees, as I spoke Arabic. That had been a whole year ago, and I had not heard a word from them all that time. What timing! The answer to my prayer, 'Now, Lord, what do I do; Jaffa is no more?' came at just the right time. What a joy to minister and work among the Syrian refugees and, in the process, practise and regain my mother-tongue, which I thought I had lost.

13

Belonging, Forgiveness and Healing

BEDFORD – 2021

Throughout my wandering years, I wonder if I have succeeded in finding my identity. Am I a Palestinian because my birth certificate says I was born in Palestine? Or am I a Lebanese because I lived for thirty-five years as a Palestinian refugee / Lebanese in Lebanon? Or am I British because the UK has given me a home and citizenship for the last thirty-eight years after my second home disintegrated? I thank God for such a privilege: for being born a Palestinian, for living and being a Lebanese and for being a British citizen. I have an identity in each, which I will carry and cherish until my dying day. My unending gratitude goes to each for giving me an identity and a home.

But did these three identities and homes provide me with that elusive inner peace and healing in my life? Yes, I found the inner peace and healing I craved through all three of my nations and homes, but I also found it through:

- *God's love and trustworthiness.* As I trusted Him in all things, He showed me His love by never letting me down. He looked after me in whatever situation I was in, in the big and in the small decisions of my life. In other words, He was my all in all. I committed my life to Him when I was thirteen, and his love and trustworthiness have been there for me ever since.

- *God's guidance,* from one country to another, providing clear direction and protection in every situation. Being on my own, I needed the assurance that He is my God. Besides guiding and protecting me, He provided the finances I needed in amazing and miraculous ways that left me in no doubt that it was He who was my provider and my protector.

- *God's forgiveness.* Through his complete pardon, I achieved perfect inner peace. I realised that I was forgiven by God's love

111

for all my shortcomings, wrongdoings and mistakes; and because of his forgiveness, I was able to forgive myself for all the pain, hurts and mistakes I made. Also, in accepting his love and forgiveness, I was able to forgive others who had inflicted suffering, hurt, anger and pain in my life and in my family's life over the years. Thereby, I found my inner peace, joy, love and freedom.

EPILOGUE

I wouldn't want to change anything that has happened to me over the past seventy-seven years. My experiences have taught me to put the Lord first and foremost in my life.

- *My identity is in Christ,* who loves me.
- *I belong* here on this earth wherever I live.
- *I have found peace,* after so many years of searching, because in forgiveness and acceptance I discovered inner joy, happiness and hope.
- *I am happy and content with who I am;* I belong and I am accepted.

A 'handful of pennies' flowed both ways. The Lord, my family and my friends have been such a blessing and so generous to me all through my life. I thank the Lord for giving me the opportunities, instances, occasions and ability to bless many others, as I was blessed.

At the beginning of this book, I dedicated my story to my praying mother, my sisters, family and friends. At the end of my story, I again dedicate this book as a testimony to Mother's God, *my God,* for being *my Father,* the father I never knew. His love surpasses all understanding.

This is my testimony regarding all that God has done for me, in me and with me; how He brought me through years of struggle fighting my battles on my own in Haifa, Beirut, London, Jerusalem, Tiberius, Ibillin and Bedford; how He has met all my needs, in the midst of trials and sorrows, and has brought me to a place of joyful contentment. I have found in Him all that I needed and will ever need every step of the way. He is still guiding, providing, healing and filling my life with his peace, joy and love. This refugee's story is my testimony to his goodness, love and dependability.

I am very pleased to say that the amount of money in the found-penny box is still £16; I have not picked up or found any more coins to put in it. You see, I do not need any more reminders to write the book. *A Handful of Pennies* was finished when I completed writing it during the Covid-19 lockdown in 2020/2021.

Thank you for joining me on my long journey. I have told you my true story. He is able to be to you as He has been to me. I just needed to know, and He just wanted to show me, how awesome and caring a God He is.

Your life and mine are not a chance happening.

Bless you.

Afaf Musallam
September 2021

SIMILAR BOOKS FROM THE PUBLISHER

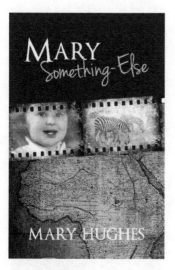

Mary Something-Else
Mary Hughes
ISBN 978-1-907509-92-6

"I want something else!" demanded two-year-old Mary.

"Well, what do you want?" her mother asked. "A sweet?"

"Yes," she replied, grabbing the opportunity, "but I want something else!"

"How about a cuddle?"

"Yes... but I want something else."

Mary's journey would take her to Africa and back, meeting many interesting people, looking for the 'something else' that would change her life forever...

Vicky's Journey from East to West
Vicky Meyer
ISBN 978-1-78815-635-6

Vicky spent her early childhood in China, during which time the Japanese Army invaded Pearl Harbour, and foreigners in China were now considered enemies of Japan. As a result, she and her school were taken to the same concentration camp as Olympic athlete Eric Liddell. After surviving the War, Vicky went on to become a stall holder in London's world-famous Portobello Road. She experienced joys and sorrows of family life, and eventually arrived in the picturesque village of Thixendale, set in the undulating countryside of the Yorkshire Wolds. Vicky's story is one of courage, hope and the faithfulness of God through all circumstances.

Available from your local bookshop or from the publisher:

onwardsandupwards.org/**shop**